LILLIAN TOO & JENNIFER TOO

2012

FORTUNE & FENG SHUI

DRAGON

D1784561

KONSEP BOOKS

ASTROLOGY . FENG SHUI . INSPIRATIONS

Congratulations!

Hi there!

Firstly, I want to thank and congratulate you for investing in yourself... and the latest edition of Fortune and Feng Shui... your personalized horoscope book for 2012! Today you have purchased one of the best possible books on the market today to guide and help you safely through the upcoming year!

What will you be earning one year from today? How will you look and feel... will you be happier and healthier in 2012?

In this little book, Jennifer and I reveal many insights pertaining to your particular animal sign...what you can expect and how to protect and enhance all areas of your life for success in 2012.

But Why Stop Here?

Now you can discover other powerful feng shui secrets from me that go hand-in-hand with the valuable information in this book. And it's absolutely FREE!

My Personal Invitation

I'd like to extend my personal invitation to you to receive my FREE online weekly newsletter… Lillian Too's Mandala Ezine. You took the first positive step to success when you purchased this book. Now you can expand your wealth luck and knowledge…and learn more about authentic feng shui that really works… including the all-important 3rd dimension of spiritual feng shui when you sign up for my FREE newsletter.

Just go to *www.liliantoomandalaezine.com* and register today! My ezine will be delivered to your inbox each week loaded with great feng shui articles, hints and tips to make 2012 your best year ever.

IT'S EASY! IT'S FREE! IT'S FRESH AND NEW EACH WEEK!

Don't miss out! It's easy to register at *www.lilliantoomandalaezine.com* and you'll also receive a special BONUS from me when you register today!

All the best,
Lillian

P.S. Lillian's online FREE weekly ezine is only available to those who register online at *www.lilliantoomandalaezine.com*

P.P.S. Ezine subscribers also receive special offer, discounts and bonuses from me throughout the year!

Fortune & Feng Shui 2012 DRAGON
by Lillian Too and Jennifer Too
© 2012 Konsep Lagenda Sdn Bhd

Text © 2012 Lillian Too and Jennifer Too
Photographs and illustrations © WOFS.com Sdn Bhd

The moral right of the authors to be identified as authors of this book has been asserted.

Published by KONSEP LAGENDA SDN BHD (223 855)
Kuala Lumpur 59100 Malaysia

For more Konsep books, go to www.lillian-too.com or www.wofs.com
To report errors, please send a note to errors@konsepbooks.com
For general feedback, email feedback@konsepbooks.com

ISBN 978-967-329-080-2
Published in Malaysia, August 2011

for more on all the recommended
feng shui cures, remedies & enhancers for

2012

please log on to

www.wofs.com

and

www.fsmegamall.com

DRAGON BORN CHART

BIRTH YEAR	WESTERN CALENDAR DATES	AGE	KUA NUMBER MALES	KUA NUMBER FEMALES
Earth Dragon	23 Jan 1928 to 9 Feb 1929	84	9 East Group	6 West Group
Metal Dragon	8 Feb 1940 to 26 Jan 1941	72	6 West Group	9 East Group
Water Dragon	27 Jan 1952 to 13 Feb 1953	60	3 East Group	3 East Group
Wood Dragon	13 Feb 1964 to 1 Feb 1965	48	9 East Group	6 West Group
Fire Dragon	31 Jan 1976 to 17 Feb 1977	36	6 West Group	9 East Group
Earth Dragon	17 Feb 1988 to 5 Feb 1989	24	3 East Group	3 East Group
Metal Dragon	5 Feb 2000 to 23 Jan 2001	12	9 East Group	6 West Group

CONTENT

CHAPTER 1.
Dragon Year 2012 - General Outlook

Transformational Energies
Bring a Year of Far-reaching Changes

CHAPTER 2.
Luck Of The Dragon In 2012

Fortune Prospects & Energy Strength

CHAPTER 3.
Personalising Your Feng Shui Luck In 2012

Individualised Directions to Protect Your Good Feng Shui

CHAPTER 4.
Relationship Luck For 2012

The charisma of the Dragon works special magic on all who meet you

CHAPTER 5.
Analysing Your Luck In Each Month

CHAPTER 6.
Powerful Protection Of Your Luck With Tien Ti Ren

YEAR OF THE
WATER DRAGON 2012
A Transformational Year

Those born in the Year of the Dragon, this is YOUR year. But you will find that the year will exhaust you as many things will happen at both a macro and micro level that will have a transformational impact on you. Developments are colored by the powerful presence and strength of the Dragon, the Zodiac system's most powerful sign. Being born a Dragon, you live with this label, but just as this can bring you soaring up high, it can also cause you some hard thuds when things fall flat.

This year 2012 is the year of the Water Dragon and it is going to be a transformational year with both positive and negative manifestations of quite extreme luck. The stars of the annual paht chee together with the patterns of element relationships bring early indications that what is in store for many of us this year will be far-reaching and life-changing.

For those born in the year of the Dragon, feng shui winds alas bring the powerfully negative five yellow star of misfortune! Luckily for you, your intrinsic element is **Yang Earth**, which does make it a little easier to cope with this affliction. But although the Dragon-born's Life Force is good, it is not overly strong. Of some concern however is the Dragon's chi essence which is weak this year. This needs strengthening, so spiritual feng shui is significantly important for the Dragon this year.

First, note the 3 stars influencing the energy of the year.

The *Star of Aggressive Sword* makes an appearance, so there is a great need to be wary. Violence in the world has not abated. There continues to be an air of collective anger pervading the world's atmosphere, which continues to find an outlet.

Interestingly also, in the 2012 paht chee chart, the Tiger continues to be around and it is a strong Water Tiger that complements the year's Water Dragon. With Tiger and Dragon present in the chart, and the **Rooster** as well (which symbolizes the Phoenix and is the Dragon's secret friend), we see the presence of three celestial guardians as well as the powerful hand of heaven. It is a year when destinies play out with brutal efficiency and big transformations take place.

This is confirmed by the number 6 in the center of the feng shui chart. Heavenly energies rule this year.

Cosmic forces are extremely powerful in 2012 and the best way to ride the Dragon Year, the most effective way to emerge stronger and healthier, happier and richer this year, is to rely greatly on powerful cosmic guardians.

And to always wear symbols of victory!

It is a year when wearing protective powerful mantras and syllables on the body can mean the difference between sailing through the year safely or becoming some kind of victim. Protection and enhancers are important aids to ride the Dragon in 2012. It is beneficial to learn subduing rituals that ward off bad luck vibes bringing violence, and to have powerful symbols of protection and enhancement in the home. This is as true for you as it is for all other signs.

Put on protective amulets that touch the energy vortexes of your throat, your heart and near to the navel where your body's central chakra is located, and where all the "winds" of the body's channels converge.

Strengthening the chakras of the human body system enhances attunement to the environment. We are currently living through a time when the energies of the world are in a state of flux. Staying protected and in sync with the disturbing energies of the environment is not difficult and is worth the small effort involved.

The year 2012 also brings the star of the *External Flower of Romance*, a star which fuels potentially painful passions. Those hit by it and engage in affairs out of wedlock are certain to create hurtful waves and aggravations in their lives! Relationship woes could well escalate in 2012; it will be worse than last year and no one is immune.

It is wise to take some strong precautions. Bring good feng shui protection into the bedroom and be particularly conscious of auspicious sleeping directions that protect the family and your marriage relationship this year. Also put into place safeguards that protect your particular love relationship.

For the ambitious and for those determined to succeed, the year also brings the *Star of Powerful Mentors*. For the Dragon in its prime i.e. the **36 year old Dragon**, your birth chart has the vital Fire element (which is missing this year) and this brings you the auspicious luck of influential people turning up in your life to give you strong and meaningful support. In 2012 you benefit from your older associates who can act as mentor figures in your professional life.

The support of such mentors could well mean the difference between failure and fabulous success. And due to the presence of the *Mentor Star* in the year's pattern of influences, it benefits for you to activate mentor luck in your life this year.

Compass directions & locations of sleeping areas must be correctly monitored this year; and the symbol of the Crystal Globe with Dragon perched at the top ascending towards the Universe attracts all-important Heaven Luck.

We have designed a very special crystal globe to be placed in the center of homes especially for this purpose - to act as a catalyst. This Dragon sitting on top of the crystal globe adds much towards enhancing the energy of the Dragon's home & work space.

It is also a year to take note of the luck of different months so that your luck is properly fine-tuned. Stay alert to all your good months; these are times when you can be confident and when opportunities will come to you. Troubled months are when you should refrain from making big decisions or embarking on any important journeys; those are times to put suitable remedies in place so that whatever setbacks, illness or disappointments make their way to you will be minor.

This series of *Fortune & Feng Shui books* for the twelve animal signs of the Lunar Zodiac is written based on studies made into the year's Paht Chee and feng shui charts. Information in these charts are combined with Flying Star feng shui, the 24 Mountains Compass Stars cycle and the Tibetan Wheel of Elements, to bring you accurate readings on what to expect for the coming year.

We go to great lengths to analyze the charts and research the cures so that we can incorporate powerful feng shui and astrological recommendations. Our philosophy of practice is that bad luck should always be effectively averted and good luck must always be strongly activated to manifest. So these books are not mere passive readings of luck.

This year we focus on the importance of house layout design and feng shui directions, as these appear to offer the best ways of taking fullest advantage of the Dragon, Tiger and Phoenix celestial presence in the paht chee chart. This is an auspicious configuration which has the potential to channel heavenly good fortune your way.

So included within is advice about placement of symbolic objects that have a celestial connection. Placed correctly within the home, they act as catalysts to luck, thus facilitating your journey through the year ensuring you sail through relatively trouble-free.

The big thing for 2012 is the power of the Blue Dragon and the great importance of Fire energy, because Fire is missing in this year's chart. The presence of Fire will instantly improve the luck of any space. This is a year to invest in bright lights and candles.

The presence of **crystal/glass globes** and **wish granting jewels** in the center of the home will also be especially auspicious, as this brings the luck of increasing wealth. In 2012 the element that signifies prosperity is the Earth element, so having **crystal balls** on your coffee tables, especially those embellished with auspicious syllables and prosperity sutras, are sure to offer excellent harmonious relationship luck.

These books are meant to assist readers to understand how their astrological and destiny luck can be improved with good feng shui in this important transformational year of the Dragon. Recommendations are based on calculations and interpretations of the charts, and analysis has been simplified so that the advice given is easily understood. Even those with no previous experience with feng shui or fortune enhancement practices will find it easy, fun and ultimately very effective using astrology and the placement of symbolic objects to improve their luck.

This book on the Dragon's fortunes for 2012 is one of twelve written specially for each Zodiac sign. It offers almost a recipe-type easy approach to preparing for the year ahead. If you find it helpful for yourself, you might also want to monitor the luck pattern of your loved ones. Who knows how good advice given within may be just the thing to jump-start their auspicious fortune, causing it to ripen! This is YOUR very own

Dragon Year when everything good or bad will seem to be larger than usual in magnitude and definitely transformational in effect. It is worthwhile taking some trouble to ensure that the year's energy syncs beautifully with yours.

GENERAL OUTLOOK FOR THE YEAR

There were severe earthquakes, floods, storms, forest fires and volcanic eruptions in the past two years, creating a disaster-driven scenario which last year was compounded by the severity of violence and civil conflicts in many of the world's troubled countries.

The last two years 2010 and 2011 saw troubled times brought by the clash of stem and branch elements, not just in the important year pillar, but also in all the other pillars.

These paht chee chart indications brought suffering and loss on a global scale, and in the immediate past year, they manifested in different parts of the world with frightening reality.

The violence that erupted in the countries of Northern Africa and the Middle East were scary but so were city shattering earthquakes, widespread floods, gigantic storms, volcanic eruptions and terrifying tsunamis, all of which started towards the closing months of 2010 and continuing into 2011. These seem to lend credence to the highly publicized end of world predictions for 2012.

Yet happily, amidst all the natural disasters and violence that have occurred, those who stayed safe also went on to enjoy good times and good news. This was because the year 2011 also benefited from powerful feng shui winds and enjoyed windows of good fortune brought by quite a good number of big and small auspicious star energies from the 24 Mountains compass stars.

So although the destiny chart of elements of the past couple of years did bring turbulent times and conflicts to many parts of the world, these discordant energies told only half the story.

On a micro basis many were able to seize the opportunities that manifested during the past year. For 2012, Chinese Astrology does not predict an end of world scenario. But will we see an end to the disaster scenario of the past two years? The charts suggest a slowing down.

2012 is the year of the powerful Water Dragon, so from an element perspective, it benefits those of you born in the year of the Wood Dragon - for you, wealth potential is at its peak! So all you **48 year olds**, you really have an abundant year ahead for you! This year is also especially beneficial for Earth Dragons. The Earth element subdues the Water element, and Earth also signifies wealth luck this year. This brings money luck to the **24 year old Earth Dragon**!

Meanwhile the astrological indications of the year are predicting a transformational year. There are however absolutely no signs of the physical world coming to an end, but the charts do point to a time of great upheaval - brought about by the natural disasters of past years - and also rather awesome change. The world as we know it continues on a path of transformation started two years ago, and gathers momentum in 2012.

These changes, which are political as well as economic, will impact the lives of many people and change the balance of influence and power in the world. But the good news is that it is also a year of renewal - at least the beginnings of good times ahead - of seeing the light at the end of the tunnel.

The Dragon year always symbolizes an apex of change. It is the celestial creature of Spring so a year ruled by the Dragon is always a time when the world will experience new beginnings in multiple dimensions of existence. The 2012 Dragon will see many countries changing directions in terms of allegiances and economic emphasis. New leaders will also emerge and violence could precede or follow upon such change.

Commercially, the world becomes more competitive and demanding. Relationships are edgy and there is an absence of general goodwill. This is due to the preponderance of yearly conflict stars. And there is also the influential *Aggressive Star* hanging over the year's paht chee.

So although natural disasters and severe fallouts caused by weather changes reduce in severity, human conflicts continue to escalate. Tolerance among world leaders is almost nonexistent so we shall hear the rattling of threats and the smell of war. This is compounded by the clashing elements in the year pillar of the Dragon - when Earth clashes with Water - so conflicts do not get resolved. Happily for mankind, this is not a fierce clash. Here, it is Earth stabilizing Water rather than Metal destroying Wood.

Besides, it is a year when the presence of the *lap chun* brings the promise of potentially good growth.

When growth energy is as strong as it is in this new year, it brings a good harvest, so symbolically, this is a very encouraging sign. Also, there is ONE pillar of the paht chee chart that shows a productive relationship between the elements, that of **Yang Water producing Yang Wood** in the Month pillar. This gives hope of rejuvenation.

The year also sees the heavenly lucky 6 in the center of the feng shui chart and this brings auspicious luck from above. Engaging the energy of tien or heaven is the key to staying in perfect sync with the year and is what will unlock good fortune luck. This involves inviting cosmic deities into the home.

This is also a year blessed by the presence of three celestial creatures - the **Dragon, Tiger and Phoenix** (the presence of the Rooster in the year's chart signifies the phoenix) and these bring very welcome powerful and protective energies. Astrologically therefore, this is a much better year than last year in terms of planting new growth and reaping good harvests. The energies of the Dragon Year are conducive to new ideas and new ways of improving oneself. Investments can be made on healthy foundations and prosperity can be nurtured.

THE PAHT CHEE CHART OF 2012

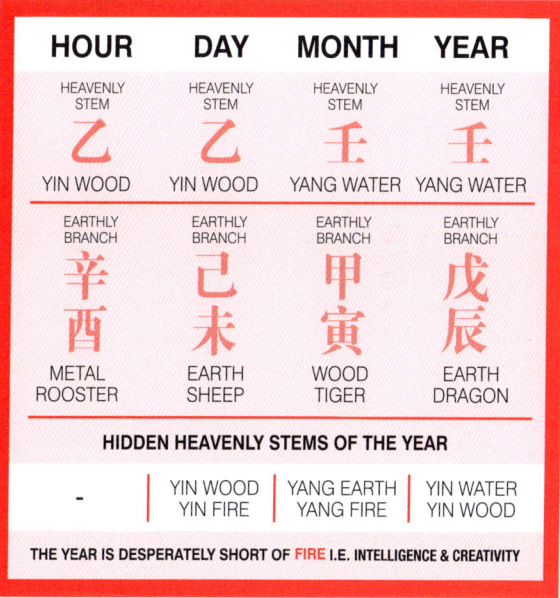

HOUR	DAY	MONTH	YEAR
HEAVENLY STEM	HEAVENLY STEM	HEAVENLY STEM	HEAVENLY STEM
乙	乙	壬	壬
YIN WOOD	YIN WOOD	YANG WATER	YANG WATER
EARTHLY BRANCH	EARTHLY BRANCH	EARTHLY BRANCH	EARTHLY BRANCH
辛 酉	己 未	甲 寅	戊 辰
METAL ROOSTER	EARTH SHEEP	WOOD TIGER	EARTH DRAGON

HIDDEN HEAVENLY STEMS OF THE YEAR

-	YIN WOOD YIN FIRE	YANG EARTH YANG FIRE	YIN WATER YIN WOOD

THE YEAR IS DESPERATELY SHORT OF FIRE I.E. INTELLIGENCE & CREATIVITY

The Four Pillars chart of 2012 reveals not just the general trends of the year but also gives a helicopter view of what can be expected in terms of trends and opportunities. The chart comprises a basket of eight elements that influences the luck of the year.

The composition of this basket of elements - Fire, Earth, Metal, Water and Wood - and the frequency of the appearance of each in the chart is what shows us what elements are missing, which are in short supply and which are in excess.

We also analyze the chart to determine the stability of the year's energies and we go deeper to look for hidden elements that bring additional inputs to the year.

The 2012 chart has only four of the five elements, so it is incomplete - there is one element missing. The missing element is **Fire** which instantly suggests to anyone who understands the vital importance of balancing the elements that everyone's home will benefit from extra lighting during the coming Dragon year. Keeping the home well lit instantly enhances the energies of any home, bringing a more auspicious foundation for the year.

It is beneficial to install more lights, keep curtains to a minimum and to literally bring the sunshine in. The Fire element in 2012 signifies intelligence and creativity, and there is a shortage of this during the year, so bringing well thought out ideas to any situation improves the success equation.

It is the clever and the wise who will ultimately prevail this year. So curb your impulses and always think things through before making important decisions.

Happily there are two hidden Fire elements in the chart and this makes up for the lack of Fire in the main chart. This is a good sign, but hidden Fire can also mean Fire erupting, so there will continue to be calamities associated with hidden Fire. Meanwhile, looking deeper into the chart, we see that there is more than enough Wood and Water energy in 2012. In fact, Wood energy is very strong, and could even be too strong. This suggests a degree of competitiveness that can turn ugly; excess Wood makes everyone more combative and scheming than usual. Neither friends nor allies are particularly helpful to each other. The hard-line impulses of the year's energies tend to be pervasive, so for the next twelve months, it is a case of every man for himself being the rallying cry.

There is also very serious jostling for power and rank in many people's lives. Especially amongst leaders, people in charge, and those who supervise others… their motivation will mainly be to outdo and outperform whoever is identified as the challenger. Success this year has to be achieved against this very competitive scenario. It plays out on any scale, macro or micro, from the smallest office situation to the global world stage; in the playing fields or in the workplace.

The energy of the working world tends to be antagonistic and hostile, fueled by the presence of the *Aggressive Star*. Words spoken will be louder and more forceful and especially between those at the top. Amongst patriarchal people, many will tend to be extra territorial, more assertive and very definitely more uncompromising. This attitude of belligerence will be the main obstacle to harmony this year.

Amongst the four pillars of the chart, you can see that three of them have clashing elements.

In the Year pillar, the heavenly stem of Yang Water clashes with the Earthly branch of Yang Earth. Here the heavenly stem energy is subdued by the earthly branch. The Dragon's earthly influence will be strong.

In the Day pillar, the heavenly stem of Yin Wood destroys the Earthly branch of Yin Earth. Here, the heavenly stem prevails. The Sheep essence here is subdued by heavenly energy.

In the Hour pillar, the heavenly stem of Yin Wood is destroyed by the Earthly branch of Yin Metal. We see here the earthly strength of the Rooster.

With 3 out of 4 of the pillars clashing, the year will not be peaceful. Harmony is a hard commodity to come by. But note that in the Month pillar Yang Water enhances Yang Wood. This is very auspicious as this means there is implied growth energy during the year.

WEALTH LUCK IN 2012 is signified by the element of Earth and with two of these in the main chart as well as one hidden Earth element, there is wealth luck during the year. It should not be difficult for wealth luck to manifest or to get enhanced. What is great is that in the hidden elements of this Month pillar, we see the presence of Fire enhancing Earth.

This is a good sign and since it is the Month pillar, it benefits those who undertake wealth-enhancing activities during the months that are favorable for them. So do make an effort to remember your lucky months during the course of the year.

Getting your timing right is often the key to making good decisions.

For the Dragon person, the lucky months for engaging in prosperity enhancing activities are the months of July and September. These two months are when you will benefit from auspicious luck coming your way.

RESOURCE LUCK IN 2012 is represented by the element of Water. There are two direct Water and one hidden Water in the chart and once again, this is a good sign as it means there will be enough resources to keep the year's growth energy stable and strong. In paht chee readings, emphasis is always placed on the stability of good luck manifesting. This year, Water ensures that the intrinsic Wood energy of the year is kept constantly nourished. The resource availability situation appears good. This also suggests that the price of oil will not be so high as to cause problems to world economic growth.

The main danger is that there might be excess Water. Too much Water can create an imbalance, in which case it should be balanced by the presence of Fire energy.

The clever balancing of elements in your living space is the key to attracting and sustaining good fortune, so make an effort to increase the presence of Fire energy in your living and working spaces.

Use red scatter cushions and red curtains, and enhance your lighting this year!

POWER LUCK IN 2012 is represented by the element of Metal and in the chart there is one occurrence of Metal represented by the earthly branch of the Rooster sign. That there is only a single occurrence of Metal suggests however that power luck in 2012 is not strong; that it is in the Hour pillar means power chi comes more towards the end of the year, and power this year is held by the young person.

The year favors power that is exercised by the younger generation of the family, and more effective when wielded by females.

What is very encouraging is that the Rooster and Dragon are *Secret Friends* of the Astrological Zodiac. The presence of this auspicious pair of celestial creatures in the year's Paht Chee bodes well for the beginning and end of the year. Their joint presence also subdues to some extent the conflict energy of the year.

The presence of the 3 celestial protectors - the Dragon, Phoenix and Tiger appearing together in the chart is also another good indication. These are three of the four celestial guardians of any space. They signify that protector energy is present during the year and to make the energy complete, it is very beneficial in 2012 to invite in the celestial Tortoise.

In 2012, all homes benefit from the presence of the **Celestial Tortoise**. Inviting an image of the tortoise into the home is beneficial and timely. Better yet is to start keeping some live tortoises or terrapins. Doing so completes the powerful quartet of celestial guardians in your home.

In 2012, the presence of an image of a tortoise is extremely auspicious for all households. It completes the celestial quartet of 2012

INFLUENCE OF
THE PAHT CHEE STARS

In 2012, we see the presence of three powerful stars in the Paht Chee chart. These bring additional dimensions to the year's outlook. They define the attitudes that have a dominant influence on people's tendencies and behavior. The three stars are:

▶ the Star of Aggressive Sword
▶ the Flower of External Romance
▶ the Star of Powerful Mentors

Star of Aggresive Sword

This star suggests a year of intensive aggression. It indicates the strengthening of the underdog's chi energy, so it does point to a continuation of the revolutionary energies started last year. Across the globe, there will be a rise of revolutionary fervor; people revolting against established authority.

At its zenith, the presence of this star suggests the emergence of powerful rebel leaders, or of highly influential opposition to established leaders. It suggests the emergence of people who seize power by fair means or foul. The name of this star is *Yang Ren*, which describes yang essence sharp blade that inflicts damage.

This is a star that has great potential for either very good or very bad influences to materialize during the year, although generally, the influence tends to be more negative than positive. Unfortunately in the chart of this year, the *Star of Aggressive Sword* is created by the strong Yin Wood of the Day Pillar with the presence of the Tiger in the Month pillar.

Here, note that the Wood element is strong in the chart, making the presence of the *Aggressive Sword Star* much more negative. It indicates that those emerging as leaders for the underdog in 2012 will end up being heavy-handed and quick-tempered.

They are charismatic but will also be strong-willed, conceited, arrogant, overbearing and self-centered - all negative traits that spell the potential for bloodshed and violence wherever they emerge. This is a real danger for the year!

CURE: In case you need protection against being personally hit by the influence of the *Star of Aggressive Sword*, or if you live inww a part of the world where revolution has already just occurred or where there has been a recent change of Government or where violence prevails, you will need the powerful **Earth Stupa of Protection**. This brass stupa is filled with powerful Dharmakaya Relic mantras within and has a protective amulet on its façade which specifically protects against dangers of any kind of violence around you.

The Earth Stupa of Protection is the best cure to use to stay protected against the Star of Aggressive Sword this year.

Flower of Romance (External)

The Flower of Romance is sometimes confused with the Peach Blossom Star because it addresses the subject of love. When the flower of romance is present in the Eight Characters chart, it suggests that there is genuine love and caring between husband and wife.

But this is a star that also reveals the occurrence of extramarital affairs. The differentiation is made between internal romance and external romance, with the latter implying the occurrence of infidelity.

The Flower of Romance Star indicated in this year's chart is that of external romance, so it suggests the occurrence of infidelity within long term love relationships, causing problems and heartaches. Marriages suffer the dangers that this year's flower of romance star poses. It is thus really helpful to wear or display the safeguards that protect the sanctity of love relationships.

In 2012 the external flower of romance is created by the earthly branch Dragon in the Year pillar and the earthly branch Rooster in the Hour pillar.

CURE: To combat this serious affliction during the year, those of you worried about infidelity in your marriage or have cause to suspect your partner of harboring thoughts of infidelity, we suggest you either wear the amulet which protects against third party interference in your relationship (and this is very powerful) OR you can also invite in **the image of a Dog & Rabbit** to counter the affliction. This subdues the possibility of infidelity causing problems for you. The Dog/Rabbit presence will create a special "cross" with the Dragon/Rooster affliction in the year's chart.

Star of Powerful Mentors

Chinese Astrology makes much of "mentor" luck, and in the old days, having a powerful patron looking after your career path at the Emperor's court was an important success factor. The prospects facing young scholars hoping to rise to powerful positions at the Court of the Emperor was always enhanced with the help of someone influential.

In modern times, it is just as excellent to enjoy the luck of being supported, helped and guided by powerful benefactors. Indeed, success often comes from "who you know rather than what you know."

37

In 2012, the presence of the Star of Powerful Mentors emphasizes the importance of Mentor Luck, so that those having someone powerful to help them in their professional or business career will have the edge in terms of attaining success.

ENHANCER: To attract Mentor Luck into your life, display a large statue of **Kuan Kung, the God of Advancement and Wealth**, in the front part of the home or in the Northwest corner of the home. The presence of this proud Taoist deity is believed to attract into the home the powerful support of a patriarchal figure that will bring good influence to the lives of those about to embark on a career. Kuan Kung also protects against violence that may harm the patriarch!

Kuan Kung, the God of Advancement and Wealth, enhances the Star of Powerful Mentors. Invite him into your home to ensure you get all the help that you need to achieve success this year.

THE FLYING STAR NUMBERS OF 2012

The Flying Star chart of 2012 is dominated by the auspicious heavenly star number 6 in the center. This is a strong star. It brings a multi-dimensional manifestation of unexpected good fortune, especially when it gets activated.

Activating any good flying star in any year is part of practising time dimension feng shui. There are three effective ways of putting this energy to work for you, all three of which are done with the intention of attracting yang chi into the part of the home which houses the auspicious "star number", in this case the number 6 in the center of the home or the center of any room.

The three methods of activating yang chi are:

Firstly, create noise...

with a radio or television placed here in the center.

Secondly, create activity...

by having a sitting arrangement here. Human energy is most powerful in activating the chi.

Thirdly, create light...

place a bright light in the place where the 6 is located. In 2012, this has a double benefit, as Fire energy, represented by light, is what brings excellent balancing feng shui.

When energized in any of these three ways, the number 6 will be activated to bring good energies into the home. It is also possible to enhance this star number further by placing powerful Earth element energy here in the center of the home. Earth element magnifies the power of metallic 6 so having crystal or glass balls on a coffee table in the center of your living room area would be most auspicious indeed. The best is to have at least a couple of crystal balls that have either auspicious images, mantras or sutras lasered on to the crystal. Or to display a large crystal ball that is beneficial to your Dragon sign.

Remember that crystals are a very effective empowering medium and above all things, crystals bring harmony and a sense of loving kindness in to the home. So this is something we do recommend strongly.

Displaying **six smooth crystal balls** (around 2 to 3 inches in diameter will do, although it is often good to have one super large crystal ball amongst the 6) always brings harmony and enhances loving energies. In 2012 this is one thing that would be extremely beneficial to bear in mind.

In 2012, it is also a great idea to activate the power of Fire element inside the home as this element, which represents intelligence & creativity, is missing from the feng shui chart. Enhancing the home with strengthened Fire will activate the good star numbers of the chart. You can do this by introducing a red crystal ball placed amongst the rest of them on your coffee table.

You can also add more light into the heart of your home. Consider installing brighter light bulbs or bringing in white lampshades that create pockets of lit up area through the spaces of your home.

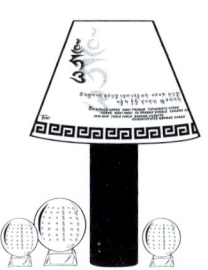

We have designed an especially auspicious **Hum lampshade** inscribed with the wishfulfilling mantra which is extremely beneficial to place in the center of your living room. Turning on the light each evening will energize the attributes of the Hum syllable and also empower the mantra.

Also add extra light to the Southwest corner of the home. Adding to the brightness of the SW sector of the home strongly enhances the matriarchal energy while subduing the hostile star number 3 which flies there in 2012. This will strengthen the mother energy of the home, which benefits the mother figure of the family and these benefits extend to the entire family.

Increase Your Lighting

If you want to really benefit from the year, you can increase the number of lights that you keep turned on at nights. It is during the night time, during the yin phase of every 24-hour day, when darkness fills your home, that you can actually counter the darkness with light!

Remember that darkness is the absence of light. So merely turning on the light dispels the darkness. It is as easy as this. Yet for so many people, it just does not occur to them; or the thought of keeping their night times lit up is just something that is strange for them.

So in 2012, because of the absence of Fire, just turn on more lights in your home, keep more lights turned on during the night times, and finally, increase the wattage of your lights. Just doing this is sure to jump start the clarity and strength of all your good fortune energies manifesting.

THE FLYING STAR CHART OF 2012

SE	S	SW
5 Yellow **5** TAI SUI	3 KILLINGS **1** Victory Star	Quarrelsome Star **3**
E **4** Scholarly Star	**6** Heavenly Star	**8** Auspicious Star W
9 Future Prosperity	**2** Illness Star	**7** Violent Star
NE	N	NW

The chart shown reveals how the nine numbers of the original Lo Shu square are laid out in the different sectors of the home for 2012.

This is probably the best way to understand the feng shui pattern of the year, as it shows how energy congregates within any built-up structure. The nine numbers laid out as shown should be superimposed onto the layout plans of homes and offices in order to understand the luck of sectors, corners and rooms in the home or office.

Every level of the home is affected by the chart, so it is necessary to superimpose the chart on every floor level of your home/office.
Each of the numbers carries energy which can be auspicious or unlucky.
The numbers have an intrinsic meaning which reflects luck patterns congregating in each of the different compass sectors of the home.

Feng shui practitioners are familiar with all the afflictive and auspicious natures of the nine numbers; and lineage texts on feng shui offer specific ways of subduing the bad numbers and enhancing the lucky numbers.

This is basically how the feng shui of homes are updated and improved each year. It is a method that has not failed, so each year, the updating procedures to ensure feng shui continues to be good requires the chart of the year to be analyzed and acted upon.

Enhancing the 6 in the Center

The most important thing to do first is to strengthen the center number 6, which is auspicious, and this we have already done by increasing lights in the center and displaying Earth element energy here with **crystal balls** or other auspicious images made of crystal.

If you can afford them, you can display **crystal images** that have **genuine 24 carat gold** embedded within. This is extremely lucky for the everyone within the household and also attracts wealth and prosperity luck for the family.

Strengthening the 1 in the South

The victory star 1 flies to the South, bringing good fortune success luck to bedrooms located here in 2012. So if you sleep in such a room, you will enjoy the luck of victory and success. You can also place the **image of a Horse** here, as the Horse brings the hidden powers of courage and endurance to the South. You can do this even though you are born in the Dragon year.

Displaying the **Banner of Victory** in the South corner of the living area or having a **small water feature** here are other excellent ways to cause the power energy in the home to manifest. This will be especially beneficial to the young women of the family - i.e. the daughters of the family.

Activating the 8 in the West

All those whose bedrooms are located in the West sectors of their home will benefit from the powerfully potent number 8 star, which flies into this corner in 2012. Here, the auspicious effect of the 8 star is strongly magnified by the *Yi Duo Star* which has also flown here brought by the compass stars of the 24 Mountain directions.

The 8 star also benefits all those whose main entrance door into their homes are located in the West sector of their home. You can then enhance the foyer area of your home with brighter lighting as Fire enhances the earth element of the 8 star. You can also place a red crystal ball with sutra here or in your West-situated bedroom to activate the power of 8. Also try and keep the door opened as much as possible to let the energy of 8 flow in.

Note that using the Fire element to activate the 8 star also subdues the Metal element of the West. Metal weakens the Earth star 8, so having it subdued will enhance the balance in favor of the 8 star. The advice given here also benefits all those with offices located in the West part of their building.

Those looking for more things to display in the foyer to improve the auspiciousness of their abode can also place the **liu li figure 8** here; or an image of the **Phoenix**. This not only activates the West sector but also the presence of the Rooster in the year's paht chee chart.

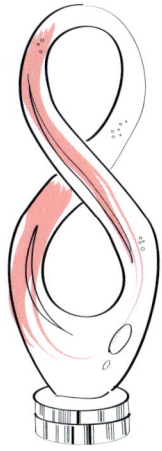

Displaying a "Figure of 8" crystal in the West part of the home or office activates "current prosperity" and fabulous wealth luck for those who live or work within.

Good feng shui is very much about enhancing the energy patterns of the home, and placement of the correct symbols in the correct corners of the home does go a very long way towards doing this.

Nurturing the 4 in the East

Contrary to what some believe, the number 4 does not bring negative connotations or bad luck under the flying star system of feng shui, and in fact, this is the number most often associated with peach blossom or romance.

Feng shui traditionalists regard this as the number which enhances the chances of marriage within families whose main entrance doors face its location, and for those whose bedrooms are placed where it flies into for the year. In 2012, the number 4 flies to the East.

The element of the East is Wood, which is in harmony with the element of 4, which is also Wood. But the energy of the number 4 star is not strong. This is because it is also affected by the *Star of Reducing Energy* brought by the compass stars of the 24 Mountains. As such, it is advisable to strengthen the number 4 star with Water element energy here.

Placing a water feature here is one way of doing this. So if your home is facing East, or if your main door is placed in the East sector of the home, having water element energy here would be very helpful in activating the positive attributes of the 4 star.

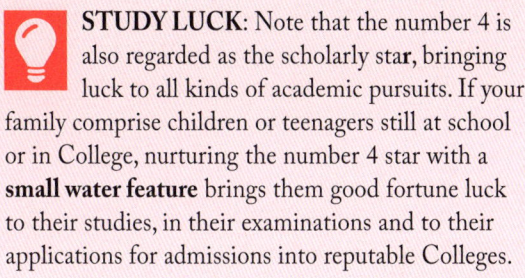

STUDY LUCK: Note that the number 4 is also regarded as the scholarly star, bringing luck to all kinds of academic pursuits. If your family comprise children or teenagers still at school or in College, nurturing the number 4 star with a **small water feature** brings them good fortune luck to their studies, in their examinations and to their applications for admissions into reputable Colleges.

It is however worthwhile noting that the water features used must not be too big, otherwise the number 4 can turn ugly, bringing the affliction of infidelity and sexual scandal. So keep the presence of water here properly balanced.

Magnifying the 9 in the Northeast

This number represents future prosperity. It is also the magnifying and expanding number which expands both good and bad. Note that the intrinsic element of 9 is Fire, another reason it is so welcome here in the Northeast. The Fire element enhances the sector's

Earth element, strengthening the energy of this part of the house. If your bedroom is located here, you will enjoy all the benefits that the number 9 brings, including the luck of permanence to all the good luck you successfully build on.

If your door faces Northeast or is located in the Northeast sector of the home, it will be very beneficial to add lights to this sector at the start of the year. Enhance the lighting of the doorway area of the home both inside and outside. Doing so will magnify the long term luck prospects of the family.

The Northeast 1 sector benefits very much from extra Fire element that gets created here. So do place extra lights in this corner; better yet, place the **Hum lampshade** or place something a bright **red** in color here - perhaps red cushions, curtains or a red dominated art piece.

ENHANCER: Anyone living in this part of any building is sure to benefit from placing bright lights here. This will attract powerful yang chi and fire energy which ensures the sector benefits form the number 9 star here.

Subduing the Illness Star 2 in the North

In 2012 the illness star 2 flies to the North, bringing the sickness affliction to all those whose bedrooms are placed in the North of their homes. And if the front door is placed in the North sector, then the effect of this affliction affects everyone living within.

The illness star is an Earth element star, and happily, its flight into the North does not strengthen it, unlike last year when the illness star in the South brought a great deal of sickness to many people.

Nevertheless, it is a good idea to subdue this affliction as it is never pleasant getting sick or succumbing to the fever bug, the coughing bug or the flu bug. Worse, the illness star weakens the resistance of all those whose life force or chi energy is not strong.

CURE: Wear the **anti-illness amulet medallion** or the protective amulet specially made to protect against succumbing to physical ailments.

Suppressing the 5 Yellow in the Southeast to Benefit the Dragon

Those familiar with feng shui afflictions know how awful the yellow star 5 can be. This is the star number that brings a whole series of bad news, illness, obstacles to success and all kinds of depressing feelings. It rarely surprises us when those affected by it start being more sensitive than usual to imagined slights, or who become extra prone to finding faults with others. One of the effects of this star is that those afflicted by it start to become really difficult to handle.

Nothing seems to make them happy, so Dragon-born people should really look at themselves in the mirror and make a real effort to be less afflicted by this star. A change in attitude will make all the difference to whether you can easily overcome whatever difficulties you face or allow yourself to be defeated by them.

In addition to the Dragon born, the Five Yellow affliction also affects those whose bedrooms or whose main doors into their homes are situated in or facing the Southeast. Do be very mindful of this affliction if it affects you.

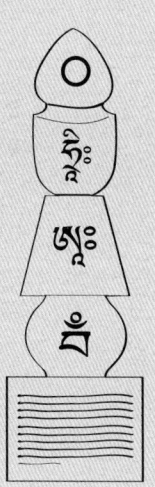

CURE FOR THE FIVE YELLOW: A good cure continues to be the **five element pagoda** embellished with the **Tree of Life** which we introduced last year. This pagoda continues to be a powerful remedy for this afflictive star.

In this Year of the Dragon however, it is also very beneficial to add the **powerful seed syllables** associated with purifying Fire energy, as this has the added advantage of engaging the spiritually powerful cures associated with these symbols.

These are the syllables *BAM*, *HRI* and *AH* which are advised in the Tibetan astrological texts for years when the fire element energy is missing. 2012 is just such a year and homes whose Southeast sectors are thus protected will stay safe from this **Five Yellow** affliction. You can also use the **Fire Element Totem Pendant** for this.

In 2012, display the Five Element Pagoda with the powerful seed syllables Bam, Hri and Ah in the Southeast.

Suppressing the Star 7 in the Northwest

The 7 star wreaked some real havoc last year, bringing violence, death and suffering to many countries in the Middle East, as well as into households whose central sector were somehow not protected against this afflictive number.

This year the number 7 flies to the Northwest, directly affecting the luck and prospects of the patriarch of households. This usually refers to the man of the family and to the leaders of countries and companies.

It brings danger of robbery and violence to those living in this part of the home; and in the office, if your desk is located here, chances are you could feel the negativity of being betrayed and let down.

Place the Blue Rhino and Elephant cure against the Robbery Star in the NW sector this year.

CURE: The best cure for the 7 star in the Northwest for this year 2012 is water energy. The presence of water near **a Blue Elephant and a Blue Rhino** would be extremely auspicious and this is because the Metal element of the Northwest strengthens the 7 star. Water is needed to weaken the Metal energy.

Subduing the Star 3 in the Southwest

In 2012, the quarrelsome star 3 flies into the location of the matriarch i.e. the Southwest. This suggests that angry mood swings afflict the mother energy of homes affecting the harmony of families and the safety of marriages. Those whose bedrooms are located here will be especially influenced by this star number.

The number 3 star is a Wood element star and is best dealt with using Fire energy.

This star number attracts the bad luck of having to cope with problems arising from the law. Court cases, litigation and quarrelsome energy will make life extremely difficult and aggravating for you if you are affected by it. If your door faces Soutwest, it is best to try using another door. You should also increase lighting in this part of the house to suppress the number 3 star.

 CURE: In 2012, the best cure for the number 3 star would be the **Magic Red Sword Diagram Mirror** which can suppress all hostile energy brought by other people's jealous intentions. This symbol is a powerful feng shui implement and is very effective for slicing through the negative intentions of others aimed at you. Placed in the Southwest, it strengthens the chi essence of the Mother figure in households.

THE STARS OF THE 24 MOUNTAINS

We also examine a third set of data which influence what the year brings to each of the twelve animal signs. These are the compass fortune stars of the 24 Mountains, which change each year.

Their influence on the luck profile of animal signs is meaningful, and working to subdue their negative influences or enhance their positive ones is an excellent way of improving one's fortunes for the year.

24 MOUNTAINS CHART OF 2012

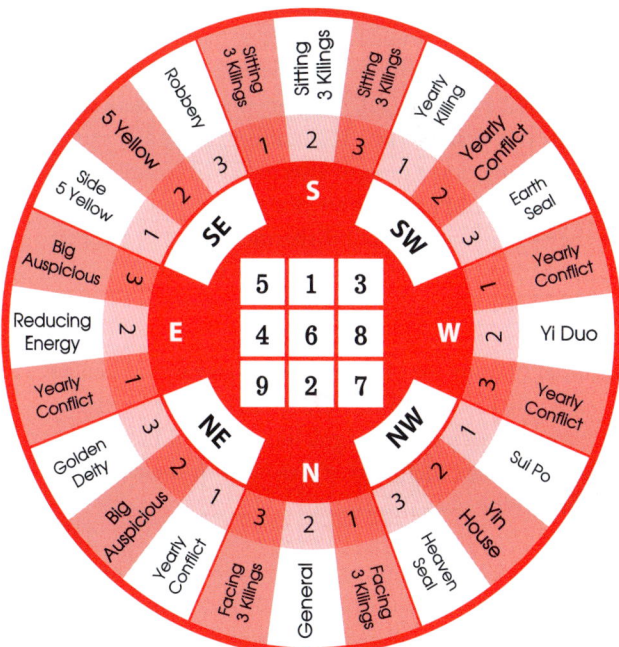

Different lucky and unlucky fortune stars fly into each of the 24 compass sectors each year, bringing energies that either increase or decrease the energy of the 12 animal signs.

There are 108 different fortune stars but only a handful fly into each of the 24 Mountain directions in any year. These bring auspicious or harmful influences, which vary in strength and type each year. The stars for 2012 are not as full of promise as they were last year. This year we see a big number of conflict stars suggesting that the signs affected are in conflict with the year. Conflict signs are not auspicious; nor do they bring anything but disharmony, so those affected should strive to use amulet or gem therapy to counter the conflict brought by the compass fortune stars.

Gem therapy uses the power of planetary influences and usually calls on activating one's favorable planets based on each animal sign's lucky days of birth - which can be their *Day of Excellence* or their *Day of Vitality*.

Animal signs that are negatively affected by the stars of the 24 Mountains should wear the "gemstone" that activates the planet that strengthens their day of vitality, and if possible, also their Day of Excellence.

So it is useful to know the gemstone to wear that will help you subdue 24 Mountain star afflictions such as conflict stars, that are stationed at or near your Zodiac sign location.

Each day of the week is ruled by one of the seven powerful planets, which can be activated by wearing the gemstone associated with the planet.

The SUN enhances Sundays and the gemstone which strengthens the energy of the Sun are all the red colored stones - rubies, rubellites and red tourmalines.

The MOON strengthens the energy of Mondays and gemstones associated with the Moon are light colored pearls (preferably white) and the Moonstone. Crystals are also good for nurturing Moon energy to strengthen Mondays.

The planet MARS nurtures the energy of Tuesdays and Mars is associated with red colored stones, although it is coral rather than any of the beryls or crystal stones that strengthens Mars.

The planet MERCURY enhances Wednesdays and gemstones associated with this planet are all the green stones, which include jade, emeralds, as well as green tourmalines.

The planet JUPITER enhances Thursdays and gemstones associated with this planet are all the yellow colored stones, the best of which are yellow diamonds and sapphires, although citrines are also excellent for pacifying Jupiter.

♀ **The planet VENUS** rules Friday and the gemstones associated with this planet are all the light blue colored stones such as aquamarines and blue topazes.

♄ **The planet SATURN** rules Saturdays and the gemstones associated with this planet are the dark blue sapphires.

Unfortunately for the **Dragon-born,** you are afflicted by the star of the *Five Yellow,* so it is extremely beneficial and even necessary to enhance your day of vitality, thus improving your energy synchronizations with that of the year. Strengthening your vitality will enhance your luck for the year and help reduce the severity of the five yellow affliction.

Note that for the Dragon, your personal lucky **Day of Vitality** is **Wednesday,** which is ruled by the planet Mercury, so wearing green jade will boost your vitality and your inner strength.

Your **Day of Excellence** is **Sunday** which is ruled by red gemstones that simulate the rays of the sun; so wearing red rubies, tourmalines and rubellites is most beneficial.

Meanwhile also note that you should never wear yellow stones or activate the planet Jupiter, as doing so brings nothing but obstacles into your life. This is because **Thursday** is your **Day of Obstacles**.

There are few things as serious as the affliction of the five yellow (also referred to by its Chinese name, *wu wang*). This is an affliction that brings serious illness, loss of profits and so forth. Its effect is similar to being hit by the *Three Killings*. Those of you with doors or bedrooms located in the Southeast should be extra wary and definitely must place the cure to subdue the *wu wang* here.

CURE: The powerful remedy against five yellow is the **five element pagoda** already referred to earlier. Because you are born in the Dragon year, you are directly hit by this star, so do place this pagoda and also the **Earth Stupa of Protection** in your home location of Southeast 1. Keeping negative energy out of such areas of the home is sure to keep your household humming along harmoniously.

Watch out for the Three Killings

More serious than conflict stars are the "killing" stars, as these bring killing energy, suggesting serious possibility of loss. In 2012, the stars of three killings bringing three kinds of loss afflict the three mountain sectors of the South. Everyone with doors or bedrooms located in the South should be extra wary and definitely must place the Cure to subdue the three killings here.

CURE: The powerful remedy against killing energy are the celestial creatures - the **Chi Lin, the Fu Dog and the Pi Yao**. Images of these three creatures newly made will have fresh and strong energy, and these should be placed in the South corners of the house and frequently used rooms that are located in the South to keep the three killings subdued.

If your staircases and corridors are located in the South, it is a good idea to place the celestials there. Staircases and corridors are conduits of energy. Keeping negative energy out of such areas of the home keeps the household humming along harmoniously.

Beneficial Signs

Two other directions benefit from the 24 Mountains and these are Southwest 3 and Northwest 3, both of which directions enjoy the good fortune of receiving **the Earth and Heaven Seals** respectively. The good thing about these seals is that if only just one member or resident of a household enjoys the support of the heaven or earth seal, based on their animal sign – in this case the **Monkey** and the **Boar** respectively – it benefits the whole household.

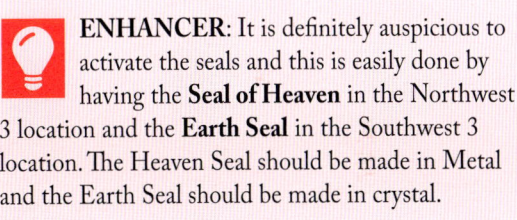 **ENHANCER**: It is definitely auspicious to activate the seals and this is easily done by having the **Seal of Heaven** in the Northwest 3 location and the **Earth Seal** in the Southwest 3 location. The Heaven Seal should be made in Metal and the Earth Seal should be made in crystal.

This year's 24 Mountains energy pattern manifests only two stars of *Big Auspicious* and these occur in the East 3 location and Northeast 2 location. Anyone whose bedrooms are placed in these two lucky directions can expect some big luck this year.

For the Dragon, the East 3 location is right next door to you on your left emanating from your seasonal friend the **Rabbit**, so this year there is the promise of *Big*

Auspicious Luck being very near you indeed! This means something exciting is just round the corner for you and it is likely to materialize in July or September for you.

Meanwhile, do remember that when your personal energy is increased, good fortune gets multiplied more easily and misfortune stars are more effectively subdued.

> The Dragon must stay strong through the year. Not many people know that it is essential to be mentally and physically strong to benefit from good fortune years that also have afflictions. Those whose mental attitudes are stable and clear always attract good fortune a lot more easily than those who give in easily to frustrations - getting weepy or angry too easily.

Some call this intrinsic confidence, and so it is, but confidence comes from having the mental strength and chi essence to stay upbeat and optimistic.

This is why a good store of yang vigor is always needed to actualize good fortune. It is your own confidence and optimism that provides the all-important missing factor, the third dimension to your luck - which is the empowerment of the self.

It is this that makes the difference between having mere mediocre luck, or enjoying truly outstanding luck. Success follows this kind of luck effortlessly. If you feel you don't have enough of it, then invoke help from the powerful deities of the cosmic realms! Here is where the practice of spiritual feng shui can be so meaningful and helpful.

Keeping Track of Your Good Months

Every year we emphasize the vital importance of timing in the way you manage your year, and in the way you ensure that the important decisions you make as well as the actions you take are made with this in mind through the course of the year. So do remember that the astrological flight of monthly stars is what brings helpful or difficult luck energy.

In these books we examine the way the monthly stars affect each of the 12 signs so that we can include detailed analysis of your luck month by month. This gives you a blueprint for when to lie low and when to strike out, and when to take risks and start projects dear to you.

These monthly analyses also highlight timely warnings that enable you to avoid accidents, avoid meeting up with bad people, getting burgled or succumbing to health risks. Good and bad months for travel are likewise highlighted.

Monthly updates analyze each month's *Lo Shu* numbers, element, trigram and paht chee luck pillars. These pinpoint your lucky and unlucky months & give valuable pointers on how to navigate safely and successfully through the year.

Aggravating obstacles can be avoided; whatever misfortune vibes that lie ahead can be circumnavigated. You can then take timely precautions either by installing remedies or by making sure you wear the necessary protection to avoid these obstacles altogether.

The monthly updates are an important component of these books as recommendations are detailed and clear cut. Through the years we have received hundreds of thank you letters from readers telling us how they successfully followed our books and reduced the impact of accidents, burglaries and illnesses.

Improving Luck
Using Compass Directions

In 2012, the use of correct facing and sitting directions - i.e. activating your personalized lucky directions - will help you stay protected against inadvertently getting hit by unlucky or disastrous transformational energies. So we have devoted a larger section this year on helping you to get your facing directions right. These are customized to assist all Dragon-born to finetune their lucky and unlucky Kua directions.

Compass direction feng shui is one of the more effective ways of making sure the energies around you help rather than hinder you, no matter what you may be engaging in through the year. The energies of the 2012 Dragon Year are strong and particularly compelling, with good and bad luck making a big impact on people's lives.

The Dragon's powerful energy needs to be controlled and managed. It is a minefield of a year in terms of belligerence and violence, anger and antagonism; these hostile vibes are strongly prevalent. It is a year when the three celestials - **Dragon, Tiger and Phoenix** desperately need the calming effect of the celestial cosmic **Tortoise**. The aura of the Tortoise is legendary

67

and having its presence can be very beneficial. But getting your directions right while sleeping, working, eating, talking and so forth will also go a long way towards safeguarding your luck this year. Do take this advice seriously.

It is really no fun being hit by bad energy; this will happen if you inadvertently face a direction that is out of sync with your sign especially when doing something important or when talking to someone important. The key is to activate directions that are lucky for you and lucky this year as well.

Spiritual Feng Shui

Finally, as something new, we are including in this year's books a whole chapter on powerful cosmic feng shui that suggests a customized amulet that is suitable for the Dragon sign to wear or display as well as the offering incense ritual to practice.

There are amulets and rituals that ward off bad luck, protect against being obstructed in your business and your career, as well as to attract specific kinds of good fortune for those building a new house, having a baby, starting a new venture, getting married, embarking on a long journey or wanting and needing cosmic assistance on a specific project. Amulets may be worn on special chakra points of the body or displayed in certain corners of frequently used rooms. This is part of the **Third Dimension of Feng Shui**, a dimension that makes the practice of feng shui much more complete.

Different animal signs benefit from different amulets, and wearing those that are best for your sign will help you to stay on top of the elements affecting you during the year.

In astrology, keeping the elements balanced is the key to unlocking good fortune, but when this is helped along by cosmic *Sanskrit* symbols and powerful mantras, the effect becomes incredibly potent as it taps directly into the power of spiritual feng shui. By bringing in the third dimension into our luck equation, we are also enhancing the feng shui of our living spaces. Space is enhanced with environmental feng shui methods through the optimum placement of furniture and auspicious objects.

Good space feng shui also means good design of layout and flow of *chi*. It takes note of compass directions on a personalized basis and uses other methods to identify lucky and unlucky sectors.

Broadly speaking, it takes care of the Earth aspect in the trinity of luck.

Time dimension feng shui address energy pattern changes over time and is founded on the premise that energy is never static but constantly changing. This means good feng shui requires regular updating by taking into account overlapping cycles of time; annually, monthly, daily, hourly and even in larger time frames that last 20 years and 60 years. It takes 180 years to complete a full 9 period cycle of 20 years.

These books address the annual and monthly cycles of change that affect everyone differently. These cycles are viewed within the larger context of the Period of 8 cycle, which deals with the heavenly cosmic forces within the trinity of luck.

Using, wearing and displaying amulets is part of the spiritual third dimension, which focuses on energies generated by mankind. In concert with cosmic forces, the strength of amulets is derived from the individual's own *yang chi*, and this is created by the mind's connections to the cosmos.

Self energy in its purest form is the most powerful kind of energy. This is Mankind Chi which combines with heaven and earth to create the trinity of luck. The empowered self generates copious amounts of positive spiritual chi and this can be directed into amulets to empower them.

When consecrated (i.e. energized) by Masters who possess highly concentrated energies through their superior practices, these amulets take on great potency.

To possess concentrated spiritual power requires years of practice; there are methods - both gross and subtle - that can be learnt which are collectively part of the inner feng shui traditions of feng shui.

In the old days, Masters of the old school were great adepts at these kinds of transcendental practice and they often made special amulets with their knowledge, to give to those who came to them for help. Some of these amulets were made according to the animal sign of birth of those asking for them.

These Masters were devotees of Taoist or Buddhist spiritual deities; many increased their own cosmic powers through regular daily meditations, reciting powerful mantras and sutras and using secret rituals to remove obstacles. In the practice of astrological traditions, the Tibetan practitioners of cosmic magic generally invoke powerful Buddhist deities who awaken within these individuals their own inner forces, sometimes bringing them to pretty high levels of siddhic accomplishments.

This aspect of feng shui, or luck invocation has only rarely been leaked out into the world. Many of the most effective methods and rituals, sutras and magical mantras are still secret, or have not yet been translated. Masters familiar with these practices reveal their secrets only to a favored few.

But already, many of these "secrets" are fast permeating city life in the great western capitals of the world - New York, London, Paris, San Fransisco and Los Angeles and so forth where shamans - or practitioners of what is being increasingly referred to as soul magic are increasingly being consulted.

We have discovered that the Tibetan way of using powerful meditation techniques accompanied by specific rituals of chanting can bring some excellent results; and particularly good for pacifying troubled energies, increasing abundance energy, controlling fierce wind energies or for subduing harmful energies.

We address some of the easier methods of doing so in the last part of the book.

The most important component of these rituals is to develop a respect for the environment around us; and also respect for the eight direction Earth Spirits who can be invoked to keep homes protected.

Some of these powerful secrets and ways of incorporating them into daily life have made their way to us. One discovery is in creating and consecrating amulets, and filling them with powerful relic pinnacle mantras as well as mantras according to the animal sign of birth.

You can also use incense offering rituals to overcome life and success obstacles. These specially formulated incense contain ingredients which many of you may not be familiar with.

But the "secrets" of offering incense that include details of the natural herbs and precious substances that are burnt as offerings to the different wind and earth spirits are aspects of Tibetan feng shui that are beyond the scope of this book.

What we have put together are compressed incense using formulations to appease local spirits and to clear obstacles that may be blocking your success luck.

For the Dragon, we recommend to use incense to clear bad luck afflictions during the months of March, April, June, August, October, December and also January 2013.

So for the Dragon-born, there are more potentially irksome months during which time you must appease the landlords and spirits of your home surroundings. Doing so engages their help and this will help you overcome all the negative indications of the charts and astrological maps for the year.

Incense rituals can remove obstacles and make your path to success smoother and a lot less aggravating.

Special amulet for the Dragon. Keeping this amulet
near you at all times will protect you from harm and from
the bad intention of others.

Chapter Two

THE DRAGON IN 2012
Luck Prospects &
Energy Strength

- Metal Dragon – 72 years
- Water Dragon – 60 years
- Wood Dragon – 48 years
- Fire Dragon – 36 years
- Earth Dragon – 24 years
- Metal Dragon – 12 years

Outlook for the Dragon in 2012

All the elements signifying the five types of luck change for the new year of the Dragon. The indications for those born in the year of the Dragon however indicate that luck for you will be a mixed bag this year as there is the strong affliction of the 5 Yellow in the feng shui chart and more significantly, your element relationships chart indicates only an average life force luck and low Chi Essence.

While it is YOUR year basically, those born under the year's sign of the Dragon need to work at being strong.

The year brings a strong does of afflictive obstacles to many of you, with much of it affecting your monetary and economic luck. The exception seems to be **48 year old Wood Dragon**, who can look ahead to some kind of financial bonanza coming this year.

The Dragon's Life Force does improve marginally over last year, but Chi Essence continues to be weak. The good news for the Dragon however is that both your Life Force and your Chi Essence do in fact see improvement over the previous year, so in terms of overall luck performance, this year will not be less than the previous year.

Nevertheless, things do not go your way very much this year. Success luck for all Dragons is quite afflicted with obstacles and setbacks, making it pretty rough for many of you. It will be quite an effort keeping yourself motivated and determined enough to keep plodding on at what you are doing - and indeed, this is a year when perseverance is the key to transforming setbacks into opportunities. Remember that it is NOT a bad year - it is just that for the Dragon, the feng shui winds are quite unfavorable and it is something that needs to be attended to, but once the particular afflictions that are causing you to lose out in the success stakes are attended to and subdued, there is no reason why you cannot depend on intrinsic Dragon energy to give you the push you need to attain success.

The ONE great indication that there could be something wonderful coming to you indirectly is the Star of Big Auspicious on your right, near to the Rabbit sign, your seasonality comrade, with whom you should therefore work closely.

Someone born in the Rabbit year will bring great benefits to you in 2012 and associating with this person will let you soak in the kind of luck that should enable you to leapfrog into a new level of success. This is a very significant dimension of your luck profile for the year & you should take careful note of this.

This year's most successful Dragon in terms of increasing your net worth is the **48 year old Wood Dragon** who can look forward to an exceptionally good year, one that brings higher and new income levels. But this increased money luck is not a result of anything that you do directly for yourself, because your personal success luck does not appear to be great. So it is likely that the financial bonanza coming your way is brought by the year's heaven luck. As such, do make sure that you enhance your personal Chi Essence this year so that you have the stamina and the spirit to "accept" the goodies coming to you. You can do this by wearing the **Enhancing Dragon Amulet** which should help you to strengthen your own *yang* essence.

The other Dragon having good money indication in its element chart is the **24 year old Earth Dragon** - it is likely that for this young Dragon, there will be stability in your finances and you too should not be having financial woes in the coming year. In fact, there could even be some positive improvement for you to look forward to.

But really, for all Dragons, this is a year to be extremely mindful of the feng shui ills that threaten to derail some of your most well-laid plans. You must make every effort to subdue and neutralize the harmful effects of the five yellow, which is a most unfortunate affliction.

79

So do make very certain that you update your feng shui placement of remedies. You have to have the **5 element pagoda** freshly filled with new earth taken from the Southeast of your garden and placed in the Southeast of your home either in the living room or in the overall Southeast of the house. Then also strengthen your personal Chi Essence by wearing powerful spiritually-enhancing sacred seed syllables made of gold - here the **Hum Pendant** - is extremely good for strengthening your internal chi which will assist you to strengthen the stamina you need this year.

The luck of the five kinds of Dragon based on the element interactions of their heavenly stems with that of year suggests the following significant summary:

Metal Dragon – Very low *chi* affects success luck
Water Dragon – A fairly stable year. Stay protected.
Wood Dragon – Unexpected financial gain.
Fire Dragon – Great health but watch your finances.
Earth Dragon – Good financial stability.

OUTLOOK FOR THE DRAGON IN 2012

The Dragon is well advised not to depend too much on its own hunches and so-called inner instincts this year as its chi essence is not at a good place. Before doing anything, it is better to analyse and think things through.

In other words, this is NOT a year to be too hasty in your decision making. For you, 2012 is a year when you will benefit very much by curbing your impulses. It is also not a year to be taking too many risks, business or personal as these will probably bounce against you.

Try to curb your natural courageous leap into the beyond and be less aggressive in pursuing fresh pastures professionally and commercially. Irrespective of where you work and what you do, whether you are a business person or working for someone or some company, this year, being circumspect and careful will pay dividends.

With weak chi essence, your "voice" lacks its usual power and authority, and it makes good sense to wait for a better time to make your presence felt. In any year, those

81

signs hurt by the five yellow will always find it a better strategy to stay low key than to be too exuberant. But all this does not mean you stop living altogether! We stress only the need to be very careful and wary especially when it comes to putting your personal assets at risk. But do note that it is not all bad luck for the Dragon.

For you, once you can successfully subdue the five yellow affliction, you can bring in ALL the enhancing symbols that will jump start your luck. Remember that there is the *Big Auspicious Star* brought by the 24 Mountains just next to you.

This is a star that advances you along promising to bring you something quite significant this year. This is good news of course, but it is better to be relaxed about it and not put too much anxiety or intensity into your expectations of it.

The promise of good luck and especially of very auspicious big luck must never be jeopardized by too much expectation.

Just be relaxed and open your mind to welcoming in something unexpected. The most likely time for this to ripen is in **July** i.e. during the summer months.

FENG SHUI ENHANCERS: To benefit from a balanced year, the Dragon can consider placing a **water feature** in its Southeast1 corner as this will help to speed up good financial luck. Water here will strongly enhance the Wood sector of the Southeast and Wood is the element that will also strengthen the inner energy which the Dragon needs.

It is also excellent for the Dragon to bring in much needed Fire energy into the home. This will ensure that the element that is missing from the chart is not in short supply in your living space. Place a **Hum lampshade** in the Northeast corner of your living room where the feng shui number of the year is the fiery 9 - activating this number here in your home will ensure that whatever obstacles may hamper you, they will stay small and will not hamper your long term luck.

Keep the lampshade turned on daily, and if you can, add some other crystal globes under the lamp as this will bring great harmony into your life. **Crystal balls** have enormous capacity to absorb afflictive vibes, especially when there is a light activating them. This should take care of the year's *wu wang* or five yellow that is hurting you this year.

Do make an effort to keep all the lights in the Northeast location of the house or living room a little brighter than usual, as this adds to the store of Fire element energy.

The Dragon sign can also improve personal life issues if it is possible to "create" a "happiness occasion" during the year. This is actually the best and most powerful way of enhancing the chi essence of your home. So those of you Dragons who are not married can consider doing so, as marriage is a big happiness occasion.

Another effective yang chi enhancer is to bring in a new baby, who can be adopted or can be a god child "borrowed" from a sister or brother. In the old days when there is a feng shui affliction and chi energy is also low, usually the person affected (if it is the family patriarch, it becomes an urgent problem) will bring in an adopted new baby. A common way of doing this is to "adopt" the child of a relative. This instantly raises the level of *yang chi* in the home!

Should there be a natural occurring *hei* occasion in your household, like your having the good fortune to welcome your very own new baby into the home, then welcome it as a very good sign indeed. The baby's pure *yang chi* - especially if it is a baby boy - it is believed, will almost instantly shoo out all the afflictive energies. You can also create such an occasion by throwing a yang evening of festivity celebrating the birthday of an older person.

As for your relationship luck, note that you will come across to others this year as being rather subdued. In 2012, you seem preoccupied and will not be overly sociable. You may also be less appreciative of other people's humor. The younger **24 year old Dragon** will be more sociable than the **36 year old**, and for all the older Dragon born, this is a year to appreciate less noisy and more contemplative pursuits.

Dragons are usually overtly competitive, and also quite aggressive, easily taking the lead and strongly encouraging others to have a good time, but this year, you will be **a lot less obvious** in your ambitions; and even for those of you who do succeed or come into some kind of inheritance or opportunity, you will stay **uncharacteristically quiet**.

This is a year when the Dragon discovers hidden strengths within itself, as it is compelled to widen its horizons and fly further afield.

The transformational energies of the year will also influence the Dragon born to rethink its life and for some of you, this could even be the year when you try out new fields of endeavor.

This can cover the entire gamut of life experiences – from travelling the world in search of adventure to enrolling for a new course of study, taking the plunge to go into politics, making a commitment to someone or changing jobs altogether.

If you feel the urge coming to you, allow yourself time to think things through using your intellect rather than your instincts. And then the benefits will come.

OUTLOOK FOR THE LADY DRAGON IN 2012

The Lady Dragon can be energetic and ambitious, benefiting from her usual vitality of spirit and creativity in looking for new worlds to conquer, but in 2012, many of you will prefer home to any place else.

You will be influenced in 2012 by your need to indulge your nesting instincts, focusing more on family and children and on your spouse, than on being out in the big bad world competing with ambitious

BIRTH YEAR	TYPE OF DRAGON LADY	LO SHU NO.	AGE	LUCK OUTLOOK IN 2012
1940	Metal Dragon Lady	6	72	Beneficial to relax and not tire yourself
1952	Water Dragon Lady	3	60	You enjoy stability in your finances & health
1964	Wood Dragon Lady	9	48	Very welcome big boost to your finances
1976	Fire Dragon Lady	6	36	Not a good time to take too many risks
1988	Earth Dragon Lady	3	24	Health & money luck bring good opportunity
1998	Metal Dragon Girl	9	12	Good recognition & results

colleagues. But only just. There will be those amongst you happy to continue pursuing life in the fast track!

The Dragon lady is forthright, brave and very capable. She takes charge easily and wears the mantle of authority without batting an eyelash. She is also pragmatic and down-to-earth. But she is less of an egoist than her male counterpart, although she can be as stubborn once she makes up her mind. In many ways, she is more tenacious in her attitudes than the male Dragon.

But in 2012, we see also a softer side to her. This can be her subconscious response to the energies of the year, or it can also be due to the instability of the elements in this year's destiny charts. There is a certain uncertainty in the year which will make her less imperious in her pronouncements.

But the female Dragon is also very pragmatic and she is able to adapt to anything. She may see herself becoming softer and gentler this year but she will have lost none of her convictions; in any case, the Dragon is a thoroughly active participant of the modern world.

She has high ideals and even higher aspirations in terms of being a citizen of the world. If given a chance, she will be an active member of protest groups and be a vocal champion of justice and equality. She has this kind of spirit, so despite a lower inner *chi* strength, she will parlay her life force towards making her presence felt within spheres of influence that interest her.

If she is the one in charge of any situation, she will have lost none of her authoritative attitude, but she is generous with those who work for her and with her.

In 2012, those interacting with the Dragon lady will find her more willing to listen. She still will not suffer fools, gladly or otherwise, but she will be less critical of those who are less capable than her.

Dragon women see themselves clearly and in a very unambiguous way. They are so focused on what they do and how they interact with others that they can come across intimidating, perhaps even unapproachable. There is a no-nonsense air about them and in the year of her own Dragon sign, she will speak her mind, although in a voice less loud and a manner less imperious.

89

In 2012, however, not all her finest qualities will be given free expression. This year, everything she does will be influenced by the transformational energy that is so pervasive during the year. But she is still a joy to be with, because she spreads her basic goodwill around. In spite of the year's low key ambience, she will not have lost her sense of humor.

Money wise, it is not an especially good year, except for the Wood Dragon, but this will not change her basic attitudes much. The Dragon woman has always been a patron of sorts, taking upon herself the role of the Matriarch. Although finances could be better and she might be stumbling a little, she will not let on to others, taking on whatever she may be called upon to bear this year all onto her own shoulders.

The great thing about the Dragon lady is her natural resilience. This will stand her in good stead this year, giving her both the faith and the fortitude to make the most of the year. And blessed as she is with the greatest of moral courage, it should not surprise anyone to see the Dragon lady surpass others - in terms of harnessing recognition and accolade for past performances - whose luck may be better than theirs. Most likely this will be the **48 year old Wood Dragon lady**!

OUTLOOK FOR THE GENTLEMAN DRAGON IN 2012

The Gentleman Dragon is usually a delightful and attractive powerhouse of energy, someone no one can ignore or take lightly. A natural leader who assumes the role of the benevolent patriarch, he is almost always the person in charge within his own peer group. But in 2012, we will see less of this and more of the careful less flamboyant side of him peeping out.

The Dragon gentleman is still very much in charge in 2012, except that this is also the year when he is more willing to give others a voice. He will make the effort

BIRTH YEAR	TYPE OF DRAGON MAN	LO SHU NO.	AGE	LUCK OUTLOOK IN 2012
1940	Metal Dragon Man	6	72	Uneventful year but stable nevertheless
1952	Water Dragon Man	3	60	Nothing very exciting but year is stable
1964	Wood Dragon Man	9	48	Recognition luck brings more money
1976	Fire Dragon Man	6	36	Staying on course despite obstacles
1988	Earth Dragon Man	3	24	Getting a good start professionally
1998	Metal Dragon Boy	9	12	Good recognition & results

this year to listen more; and to embrace the instincts and talents of others around him.

He continues to admire performance and be galvanized by successful people who demonstrate the kind of vitality he likes and admires and which he sees himself lacking this year. Because of his characteristic inbuilt antennae, as well as his own fabulous instincts of survival, he will always be aware of his own drawbacks.

The Dragon male will feel a lack of inner confidence and conviction, but rather than be floored by these realizations, it will merely spur him on to look for these qualities in others. In doing so, he will be seamlessly and almost subconsciously replenishing his own store of *yang chi*.

The Dragon male has great courage and terrific tenacity. He is impatient with those who whine and complain; to him, performance can be good irrespective of circumstances, and it is this natural resilience against bad energies that the Dragon reinvents himself.

So in 2012, the lack of good vibes around him during the year will not cause him to give in, instead it could galvanize him to be even more demanding of himself, sleeping less and working more. Working not less hard but more intensively.

The Dragon is a demanding boss, but expecting more of himself than of others. Nevertheless, he is sensitive to criticism and does not react kindly to those who disagree with him. He also does not like to negotiate and will often walk away from a deal rather than give in to those who ask for more.

> What the Dragon fears most is losing face, so ego is important to him. He is rarely the cunning strategist or crafty politician - there is an inbuilt strain of gentlemanly honor in his make-up, and what he shows to the world really is the real him.

But he does play with cards close to his chest. In short, he is demanding but not unreasonable, resilient but never fanatical and he respects those who impress him with substance. This does not change one bit in 2012 because irrespective of his personal circumstances, he stays very true to the principles by which he lives and works.

Thus in 2012 we will see the Dragon male being as courageous as ever, except this year colored by a self-imposed stricter standard of risk-taking. He is not oblivious to his own feelings of self doubt, even though he does not relate this to any loss of ability on his part. He knows he is not as confident this year, so he simply decides to be extra cautious in his decision making.

The older Dragon born gentlemen – those **72 years old** in 2012 - will be quite satisfied taking life easy, perhaps doing a bit of travelling and enjoying the grandchildren a lot more. He knows that he must take care of his health this year and that it is better not to try to achieve anything.

Dragon Gentlemen who touch **60 years** this year will enjoy a more fruitful year than his older compatriot but it is possible he too could decide to give himself a break and enjoy some of the fruits of his past labors rather than continue on in the daily grind of working life fuelled by a continuous sense of wanting to achieve and make a difference. There is no danger of loss or financial instability for him in 2012, but he too will decide to be careful about finances and risk taking.

Dragons in the prime of their career have at least one good thing to look forward to this year.

The **48 years old** appears to have excellent money luck, so this is indeed something to make the year exciting and full of promise. For the **36 year old** however, things do not look as rosy, so this appears to be the kind of year when he needs to plan and strategize, to network and forge alliances, rather than go all out looking to open new markets, or make new inroads.

The **24 year old**'s luck is also good so here we are likely to see a natural born leader testing the waters and making his frits forays into the great big world.

ENERGY STRENGTH ANALYSIS OF DRAGON LUCK 2012

The following section focuses on the element luck analysis of the Dragon in 2012. This reveals five kinds of luck in the Dragon horoscope and are charted according to how the Dragon's ruling luck elements in the year of birth interacts with the elements of the year 2012, thus offering indications of strength or weakness in the horoscope for the year for the different Dragons.

It is always a good idea to investigate your personal chi levels in any given year as this reveals your inner strength. Usually, those whose Chi Essence is strong in any year will tend to have the luck to overcome astrological afflictions much more easily. And for those sailing through a good year, the enhanced Chi Essence empowers manifestation luck so that the auspiciousness of the year gets felt even more acutely.

But this is not the case for Dragon, who in 2012 is neither having a very remarkable year nor being helped by the feng shui affliction of the five yellow. But knowing this enables the Dragon to do something concrete about correcting the situation. Check the five tables on pages 99-101 to take note of the state of your five luck categories for 2012.

The significance of the luck indications is explained as follows:

First, Your Life Force...

This highlights the hidden dangers to your life. Danger to one's life manifests suddenly and with little warning. In the past two years, clashing elements in the paht chee chart brought raging wildfires, tsunamis, floods, earthquakes and other natural disasters that wreaked havoc and destruction.

Last year, this was compounded by the feng shui chart which brought the violent star 7 to the centre, so we saw raw human anger overflow into revolution that brought danger into the lives of millions of people. Many of these uprisings and disasters happened without warning. Staying safe against being caught unawares is an important aspect of horoscope readings.

Luckily, for all those born in Dragon years, your Life Force luck shows a safe **O** for 2012 and this means that your life force is strong enough that you do not succumb to threats to your safety. So you need not worry, despite turbulence in the world's energies.

Second, Your Health Luck...

This is the luck of your health condition during the year and it indicates how strongly you can avoid illness bugs. For the Dragon, note that the feng shui chart brings bad strong winds that can cause you illness afflictions. The readings in this category must thus be viewed in this light.

Most threatened by illness is the **48 year old Wood Dragon** as you have a **XX** against your health window. - all other Dragons are stronger. When the luck indication is a double cross **XX** it means that 2012 can bring ailments and vulnerability to health issues; and these cause obstacles to work schedules. Plans get blocked and opportunities get missed. Poor health luck means you can get food poisoning easily, and you catch wind borne diseases.

You should use a cure against illness. This is either the **wu lou** or the **vase with healing nectar**. For the others and especially for the older Dragons, there is no threat to your health luck; and for the very healthy **24 year old**, you have absolutely nothing to fear at all!

The 48 year old Wood Dragon should wear or carry a Wu Lou or health amulet to counter the negative affliction against its health luck this year, and also display the Wu Lou beside the bed.

Third, Your Finance Luck...

This reveals if you will enjoy financial stability during the year. It is also an indication of whether you can do better than the previous year. This does not look like a great year for Dragon's financial luck except for **48 year old**, who enjoys bonanza via the triple **OOO**. This means very substantial gains of new wealth coming to you in 2012. The other Dragon having good money luck is the **24 year old** with a double **OO**.

The 36 year old Dragon has a **XX** against its financial luck category and this spells loss, so 2012 is a year to be careful about your economic situation. A single circle **O** means the year does not bring much change to your finances and you will enjoy a stable situation. There are few surprises to make you worry. This reflects the case of the **60 year old Water Dragon**.

Fourth, Your Success Luck...

This highlights your attainment luck for the year whether it be success in your professional work or in your studies. Circles are strong indications of success while **XX**s are negative indications suggesting obstacles. The luck indication for all of you born in Dragon years is the discouraging negative **X** indication although it is only a single cross. This means you will enjoy a highly unstable year at work. Your professional life does not flow smoothly and there will be many distractions and obstacles. As a result, success will be quite difficult to come by. People become critical of your abilities, so in terms of attainments, this is alas not really your year.

Fifth, Your Spirit Essence...

This reveals insights into your inner resilience and spiritual strength. When at a high level you have enormous power to subdue spiritual afflictions and can overcome the lack of other categories of luck. Low Spirit Essence, indicated by crosses, is negative indications. The Dragon has a single **X** against its Chi Essence, so your inner spirit is weak and unstable. This is not a good indication and you should try to enhance your personal chi by wearing **enhancing seed syllables** touching your body. These are best worn as a pendant touching your heart chakra.

The best syllable for the Dragon in 2012 is the all-powerful *Hum* seed syllable. Wear this through the year to compensate for your low chi energy.

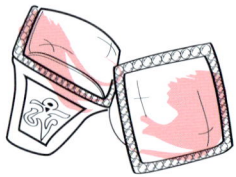

Wearing the Crystal Power Ring with the seed syllable Hum helps maintain good Chi Essence through the year, allowing you to maximize your good luck in this category of luck.

METAL DRAGON
72 YEARS OLD

TYPE OF LUCK	ELEMENT AT BIRTH	ELEMENT IN 2012	LUCK RATING
LIFE FORCE	EARTH	EARTH	O
HEALTH LUCK	METAL	WATER	OX
FINANCE LUCK	METAL	WATER	OX
SUCCESS LUCK	WOOD	WOOD	X
SPIRIT ESSENCE	FIRE	FIRE	X

WATER DRAGON
60 YEARS OLD

TYPE OF LUCK	ELEMENT AT BIRTH	ELEMENT IN 2012	LUCK RATING
LIFE FORCE	EARTH	EARTH	O
HEALTH LUCK	WATER	WATER	O
FINANCE LUCK	WOOD	WATER	O
SUCCESS LUCK	WOOD	WOOD	X
SPIRIT ESSENCE	FIRE	FIRE	X

WOOD DRAGON
48 YEARS OLD

TYPE OF LUCK	ELEMENT AT BIRTH	ELEMENT IN 2012	LUCK RATING
LIFE FORCE	EARTH	EARTH	O
HEALTH LUCK	FIRE	WATER	XX
FINANCE LUCK	WOOD	WATER	OOO
SUCCESS LUCK	WOOD	WOOD	X
SPIRIT ESSENCE	FIRE	FIRE	X

FIRE DRAGON
36 YEARS OLD

TYPE OF LUCK	ELEMENT AT BIRTH	ELEMENT IN 2012	LUCK RATING
LIFE FORCE	EARTH	EARTH	O
HEALTH LUCK	EARTH	WATER	OO
FINANCE LUCK	FIRE	WATER	XX
SUCCESS LUCK	WOOD	WOOD	X
SPIRIT ESSENCE	FIRE	FIRE	X

EARTH DRAGON
24 YEARS OLD

TYPE OF LUCK	ELEMENT AT BIRTH	ELEMENT IN 2012	LUCK RATING
LIFE FORCE	EARTH	EARTH	O
HEALTH LUCK	WOOD	WATER	OOO
FINANCE LUCK	EARTH	WATER	OO
SUCCESS LUCK	WOOD	WOOD	X
SPIRIT ESSENCE	FIRE	FIRE	X

METAL DRAGON
12 YEARS OLD

TYPE OF LUCK	ELEMENT AT BIRTH	ELEMENT IN 2012	LUCK RATING
LIFE FORCE	EARTH	EARTH	O
HEALTH LUCK	METAL	WATER	OX
FINANCE LUCK	METAL	WATER	OX
SUCCESS LUCK	WOOD	WOOD	X
SPIRIT ESSENCE	FIRE	FIRE	X

103

Chapter Three

PERSONALIZING YOUR FENG SHUI LUCK IN 2012

Individualized Directions to Protect Your Good Feng Shui

In 2012 the Dragon's fortune and feng shui is not at its best and in fact, luck for the Dragon born gets afflicted by the 5 yellow, the star of misfortune. Apart from placing powerful 5 element pagoda cures, what the Dragon can do to ensure a smooth and steady year where obstacles are kept to a minimum is simply to use good direction feng shui that relies heavily on the Eight Mansions formula and also to use element therapy to balance out the energies of the year.

Dragons in 2012 must subdue the 5 yellow as strongly as possible and the good news is that this is not difficult to do once you have access to the correct remedy which is the all metal 5 element pagoda which will keep the powerful 5 Earth Star in check. Here Metal exhausts Earth, keeping the *wu wang* or 5 yellow distracted and thus made less harmful.

The Dragon of course benefits from it being its own year. This itself enhances the Dragon's strength, enabling it to rise above obstacles and distractions that make their way to you.

The energy of the Dragon Year is favorable to its own sign, and in 2012, the Dragon benefits from an infusion of powerful annual chi energy. So the year looks sufficiently promising for the Dragon not to feel discouraged by some initial setbacks at the start of the year.

Relationships may not go smoothly at first, and there will be some confrontational energy to sort out. Best is for the Dragon to ignore provocations, keep your head low and work on steadily. Things should improve and with correct use of feng shui directions that directly benefit you, you can also transform the negatives of the year into quite spectacular success.

In terms of feng shui luck, what the Dragon can do immediately is to give the home a thorough spring cleaning, making sure the energy in all your living and work spaces are not left to stagnate. This is equivalent of five minutes of body shaking each morning, something which experts on energy highly recommend to ensure the chi within our bodies are kept moving each day when we wake up.

Shift your furniture to move your space chi. This allows air to flow through the hidden spaces of nooks and corners, and when you are done, move your furniture back. Use this exercise to clean hard-to-reach spaces. This is a powerful re-energising ritual, which encourages energy to move, thus creating yang chi and bringing vibrant new energy into the home. This is especially important for the Dragon-born, to ensure that energy associated with whatever stress or setbacks of the past year do not linger on. Flushing out the previous year's energy also revitalises the energy of the home.

In any case, this shaking and chi-moving ritual also makes sure your life does not stagnate and ensures you will successfully initiate new projects and grow with a steady and sure hand. It may sound simple but these simple rituals are very effective.

Next you can customize the feng shui of your space by activating the astrological location of your animal sign and also by using compass directions feng shui to maximise your luck for the year.

MAKING DRAGON'S SOUTHEAST 1 LOCATION AUSPICIOUS

The location of the Dragon is Southeast 1. You must know exactly where this part of your home is; this is your Dragon location which you must pay special attention to. You must never, for whatever reason at all, leave this corner dirty, cluttered or worse, filled with rotting materials.

This part of the home must reflect your care and attention and it should definitely not be your store room or your toilet, and also try not to do any cooking in this part of the house or room. It is vital to bring correct feng shui inputs to this part of the home, as well as to this Southeast 1 corner of all the rooms frequently used by you. The element of this space is Wood, while the incoming feng shui wind here in 2012 is Earth. Here note that the incoming Earth chi is unfriendly and does not bring good luck to the Dragon's sector. So it is excellent that the Wood element of the corner can subdue the Earth element of the 5 yellow.

Placing more **plants** to increase the strength of the Wood energy is even better to ensure that the feng shui of your overall home space does not suffer too much from the negative influences of the five yellow. Remember to keep this bad star 5 subdued, as under normal circumstances, it can bring about a major reversal of fortune. So it really is beneficial to be diligent in using feng shui methods and symbols to subdue this bad luck star of 5.

The Wood element energy here in the Southeast 1 sector benefits the **48 year old Wood Dragon** bringing you the luck of great financial gains.

It is definitely beneficial for the Dragon person to enhance the Wood element in all the SE1 sectors of the rooms you frequently use, as this keeps the affliction of the year strongly subdued. One thing we also want to recommend is to place a **Double Dragon water feature** here in the Dragon location of your house i.e. SE1 sector. Water will keep the Wood element strong through the year.

One of the best feng shui ways of strengthening the element of Wood is to have Water element around, so anything that creates the sound of water or has moving yang water is auspicious and thus a good idea. But if you place water here in Southeast, also place some live plants as well.

ENHANCER: Place the **Tree of Life** here in the Southeast 1 sector as this is an excellent enhancer here. The 2012 tree of life also brings wealth and prosperity luck. It is a young tree that is beneficial this year to signify the season of Spring and also to represent new beginnings - both of which are elements that benefit the Dragon.

Place the Tree of Life in the Southeast sector of the home to bring new opportunities for the Dragon this year.

ENHANCING YOUR PERSONAL LO SHU NUMBER

The Lo Shu number of men and women born in the year of the Dragon is either 6, 3 or 9. Your personalised Lo Shu number interacts with the Lo Shu number of the year and your good luck during the year is either enhanced or afflicted by the way the numbers interact.

The Lo Shu number of 2012 is the white number 6. This benefits Dragons with this Lo Shu number. The Lo Shu numbers of those born in Dragon years are shown below.

Dragon with Birth Lo Shu of 6
(affecting the 36 & 72 year old Dragon)

The number 6 gets auspiciously doubled by the number 6 of the year, and this emphasizes all the characteristics attached to this Lo Shu number affecting the 72 year old Metal Dragon and the 36 year old Fire Dragon who both have this as their birth Lo Shu number.

So in 2012, their attributes of high intelligence, help from unexpected sources and great networking luck bring them amazing big opportunities. Their business luck will also get enhanced as they start to catch the

BIRTH YEAR	ELEMENT DRAGON	AGE	LO SHU NUMBER AT BIRTH
1940	METAL DRAGON	72	6
1952	WATER DRAGON	60	3
1964	WOOD DRAGON	48	9
1976	FIRE DRAGON	36	6
1988	EARTH DRAGON	24	3
2000	METAL DRAGON	12	9

eye of important people. It also indicates that they might move into a new house this year although it would have been better done before the year changes i.e. done in the year of the Rabbit. This is not a great year to uproot yourself by moving location or country. It is also not a good year to change jobs.

If you have plans to make big changes better to wait till the following year. Protect the Southeast of your home with remedies to dissolve the influence of the 5 yellow and also place water in this corner.

Dragon with Birth Lo Shu of 3
(affecting the 60 & 24 year old Dragon)

The number 3 is softened by the number 6 which is the Lo Shu number of the year. This combination brings better diplomatic skills to the 60 and 24 year old Dragons whose dogmatism and stubborn nature can otherwise get them into trouble in 2012. The Lo Shu of 3 makes these Dragons very authoritative and strong-willed, although happily in 2012, they are more subdued.

There will be wise counsel made available to them and perhaps even an influential mentor to bring them good advice. A special word of advice to 24 year old Dragon is to curb their enthusiasm this year. There are powerful changes taking place in the world that bring unexpected new opportunities their way. It is better not to be excessively impulsive.

Dragon with Birth Lo Shu of 9
(affecting the 48 & 12 year old Dragon)

The Lo Shu number of this Dragon is 9 and its relationship with the number 6 is neutral, but both are lucky numbers that bring different aspects of good fortune luck, so this is a good and lucky year for these Dragons. The 9 with 6 is an excellent indication in terms of increasing your wealth luck. There will be unexpected developments that lead to some exciting possibilities as the 6 brings luck from heavens. So this is a year when many opportunities can manifest, but do be discerning when trying to take advantage of these opportunities. Curb your enthusiasm and always use your head over your emotional reactions.

In the euphoria of new pathways, you can succumb to carelessness and impulsiveness. But make no bones about it, the combination of 9 with 6 is very promising; just be careful not to take action without careful thought first. Protect the Southeast with a water feature and also place a bright light here. This will do wonders for your recognition luck.

Protecting Dragon's Afflicted Direction in 2012

Use a compass to determine the Dragon direction of your home, which is Southeast 1. This refers to the Southeast sector of the whole house and the Southeast corner of rooms you frequently use, such as your bedroom or home office. Make sure you do not have a toilet in the Southeast. A toilet in your Dragon direction flushes away the luck of residents belonging to the Dragon sign. Career luck is hard hit and your reputation luck can suffer. Those in business face an array of problems including financial loss.

A store room in the Southeast would ordinarily lock up your good luck potential, but since the Southeast location is so afflicted, a store room here could well do you a favor, because then the store room can lock up the 5 yellow which has flown to the Southeast.

If you envisage staying in the same home for several more years however, the long term effect of a store room here could restrict your own growth luck. If the energy of the Dragon gets locked up, you might find it hard to fly, to soar and to grow so be alert to this possibility and demolish the store room here after the year of the Dragon is over.

If you have a kitchen here in the Southeast, it is advisable to consider changing the room usage of your Southeast sector, as a kitchen here is going to block your luck. The best use of the Southeast, which is your sector, is to make sure it gets activated positively, and in 2012, the best element here would be anything that has Wood with Water energy.

When you create an active space where most of your productive work gets done, it energizes your most personally important sector of the home, thus benefiting you. Always make sure the energy here in your home location of Southeast is vibrant and active, yang in nature and never has a chance to get stale allowing *yin chi* to accumulate.

FINETUNING DRAGON'S LUCKY DIRECTIONS IN 2012

The Eight Mansions formula divides people into East and West groups, with each group having their own lucky and unlucky directions. To use Eight Mansions, you need to first determine your auspicious directions and then you should make it a point to always face at least one of your good directions while working, negotiating, sleeping, eating or dating.

There are different lucky directions for men and for women, and these are calculated using their lunar year of birth. Just doing this faithfully, using a good compass to determine the directions, will bring you instant good feng shui. This is also one of the easiest formulas of feng shui to use and the one which you are least likely to make a mistake. Study your good and bad luck directions from the charts here. Note that the directions are different for each of the Kua numbers and also note that the Kua numbers are different for male and female Dragons.

AUSPICIOUS DIRECTIONS FOR DRAGON WOMEN

BIRTH YEAR	AGE	ELEMENT/ KUA	HEALTH DIRECTION	SUCCESS DIRECTION	LOVE & FAMILY DIRECTION	PERSONAL GROWTH DIRECTION
1940	72	METAL/9	SE	E	N	S
1952	60	WATER/3	N	S	SE	E
1964	48	WOOD/6	NE	W	SW	NW
1976	36	FIRE/9	SE	E	N	S
1988	24	EARTH/3	N	S	SE	E
2000	12	METAL/6	NE	W	SW	NW

Chart showing auspicious directions for Lady Dragons.

Dragon women with Kua numbers 3 or 9 belong to the East group of lucky directions - and they benefit from facing East or South in 2012, as these are directions that are good for them and that are also not afflicted in 2012. The best direction for East group people this year - for romance and good relationship luck - is East, which has the auspicious peach blossom star of 4. This star also brings excellent scholastic luck for residents. Those of you whose success direction is South also benefit this year because South is blessed with strong victory luck in 2012. This facing direction is especially suitable for the **24 year old Dragon lady** who is just embarking on a career or in a serious relationship. For her, facing South will bring excellent relationship and success luck.

East group women Dragons should not face North as this is an afflicted direction that brings illness and general feelings of apathy and lethargy. You should also avoid facing the Southeast, which is the Dragon's own direction, because it is very badly afflicted in 2012 and is thus best to avoid this year.

The **48 year old Wood Lady Dragon** and **12 year old Metal Dragon girl** belong to the West group. These ladies should definitely tap the very lucky West direction this year as it is from the West that powerful good fortune comes in 2012.

But you must both avoid your best directions of Southwest and Northwest, because these two directions are seriously afflicted with the conflict and the cheating stars respectively. Instead, it is better to face your other good luck direction i.e. the Northeast, which benefits from the luck of future prosperity.

117

AUSPICIOUS DIRECTIONS FOR DRAGON MEN

BIRTH YEAR	AGE	ELEMENT/ KUA	HEALTH DIRECTION	SUCCESS DIRECTION	LOVE & FAMILY DIRECTION	PERSONAL GROWTH DIRECTION
1940	72	METAL/6	NE	W	SW	NW
1952	60	WATER/3	N	S	SE	E
1964	48	WOOD/9	SE	E	N	S
1976	36	FIRE/6	NE	W	SW	NW
1988	24	EARTH/3	N	S	SE	E
2000	12	METAL/9	SE	E	N	S

Chart showing auspicious directions for Dragon Men.

Advice for Dragon men is similar to that offered to the Lady Dragons. Once you know if you are East or West group, you will know which directions to tap into and which to avoid in 2012.

East Group Dragon men/boys have Kua numbers 3 and 9, while the West group gentlemen Dragons have Kua number 6. Note that those of you whose success direction is East can face East this year, and doing so brings good health and good relationship luck. It is the Southeast you need to avoid facing!

The other good direction for East group guys is South, which is also the success direction of the **60 year old Water Dragon gentleman** and the **24 year old Dragon young man**. This indicates that these two Dragons enjoy better luck than the others, as South is a winning direction in 2012. The young man especially will benefit from facing South if he is looking to find a meaningful job to get him started onto a fine career.

The West group Dragon gentleman (**72 and 36 years old respectively**) are advised to tap strongly into the West direction and to give the Southwest and Northwest a miss this year. But facing Northeast brings the luck of longer term wealth-building luck.

IMPROVING DRAGON'S FENG SHUI LUCK IN 2012

Note that the fastest way to attract good fortune is to tap your personalized lucky directions. As long as you make certain that your lucky directions are not afflicted in 2012, facing a direction that brings you good fortune and which is also in sync with the year really is the easiest way to ensure good feng shui for the year. Note that even if you cannot face or tap your best direction, you MUST at least avoid facing directions that are unlucky for you or that are afflicted in 2012.

119

Attracting Success

Dragons with Kua number 6 should position their sitting direction at work to face West or Northeast as discussed earlier. Those with Kua 3 or 9 should face South this year or East for improved relationship luck. Taking note of the directions that are best for you, try to arrange your desk to face the appropriate lucky direction; but also take note of the taboo desk alignments to avoid. To start, always look at what is behind you. Do not get hurt by something behind you while focusing on facing a lucky direction. Watch your back! So…

▶ Avoid a window behind you, especially if your office or home work area is located several levels up a multi-level building.

▶ Avoid having the door into your room being placed behind you.

▶ Avoid being directly in the line of fire of sharp edges or tables, corners and protruding corners. And definitely DO NOT place your desk at funny angles just to tap into your lucky direction. This can backfire bringing misfortune luck instead.

Personal
Growth
Direction

Do not sit with your back towards the door, as this creates the
bad feng shui that leads to gossip, politicking and backstabbing.

Ensuring Good Health

An excellent way to ensure good health in 2012 is
to capture your individual good health direction.
The secret of good health luck is to sleep with your
head pointed to your health direction or at least one
of the four auspicious directions. You should ensure
that your health direction does not suffer from any
affliction in 2012.

In this respect, Dragons should note that the two
West group directions that are hurt by the feng shui
winds of 2012 are the Southwest and the Northwest.
These two powerful directions are hurt by hostile

121

energies, so even if they are listed as your health direction, do not face these directions or sleep with your head pointing to either of these directions.

As for the Dragon men and women who belong to the East group, note that the North is seriously afflicted by the illness star, so on no account should you face North.

Likewise, the Southeast is seriously hurt by the five yellow which also manifests illness of the most severe kind. This too is a direction to be avoided. Remember that sleeping right is one of the easiest of feng shui ways to ensure good health. This plus making sure you are not afflicted by the annual and monthly illness star numbers is what will help ensure you do not succumb to sickness.

For all Dragons, please note that the months of April 2012 and January 2013 are when you must take extra good care of your health as these are the two months when you are the most vulnerable. In these two months, do wear the **gold wu lou** as this is an excellent amulet against getting sick. You can also wear the **Medicine Buddha moving mantra watch** which was made precisely to guard against falling ill to epidemics or viruses.

In the Bedroom

To enjoy good feng shui, always be sensitive to the way your bed is oriented and positioned in the bedroom. A golden rule is that beds should always be positioned against a solid wall, and should not share a wall with a toilet or bathroom on the other side. This gives you the solid support you need and the headboard forms a symbolic protective aura that guards you while you sleep. So it is always preferable to have a headboard.

You should make sure never to have toilets on the other side of the wall where your bed is placed. The toilet symbolically flushes away all bad luck and to have it directly behind you while you sleep suggests that all your good luck gets flushed away as well.

Beds that are placed against a wall with space around it are always more auspicious than beds that are wedged tight into corners. Do make sure there are no heavy beams above you as you sleep and no sharp columns hitting at you from protruding corners and cupboards. These cause illness.

And do take note of window views. If you can see blue skies at nights and there is a clear view, it is both healthy and auspicious. So also are views of vibrantly growing trees, although these should never be too near to your window. But do make sure not to be looking at a dead tree stump or a hostile looking tree outside as these can bring illness into the bedroom.

Becoming a Star at School

To bring good feng shui luck for your 12 year old Dragon, note that the boy has Kua 9 and is East group while the girl has Kua 6 and is West group. In 2012, the Dragon girl can benefit hugely from sitting facing South, which is your personal growth direction. But you can also face East because the literary and scholastic star has flown here. So for the Dragon girl, facing South or East both benefit.

The Dragon boy belonging to West group should face West or Northeast, and although this may not be the best direction to benefit from your own personal growth luck, these two directions are excellent for bringing present and future success.

Attracting Romance into your Life

If you are looking for love, there is good news for Dragons belonging to the East group, because the *Peach Blossom Star* lands in the East in 2012. This makes it a powerful love direction for activating marriage luck this year. So no matter what your age or whether you have been married before, this year you can set the energy moving to bring you good marriage luck simply by placing a **bejeweled Rabbit** in the East!

For West group Dragons, we advise to tap the West sector by placing a **bejeweled Rooster** in here because the peach blossom luck of the Dragon is the Rooster. This is a good way to jump start your marriage prospects luck. But wearing the **Phoenix scarf** will also bring romance and love your way!

For Dragons looking for love and marriage luck, wear the phoenix scarf.

125

Chapter Four

RELATIONSHIP LUCK FOR 2012

The charisma of the Dragon works special magic on all who meet you

Each year, we all react to the people around us differently, and depending on what our sign is, we can be more accommodating in one year and less so in another. How you treat and respond to those you love - your family, lovers, spouse or children - and to those you work with - colleagues, employees, bosses and business associates - depend very much on your relationship energies during the year. This will influence your tolerance levels and your patience. Some years you can be very loving and forgiving, feeling at ease with yourself and with the world, and during other years, you can be less tolerant and very impatient.

COMPATIBILITY WITH
EACH ANIMAL SIGN CHART

COMPATIBILITY	LUCK OUTLOOK IN 2012
DRAGON with RAT	A great year to inspire one another
DRAGON with OX	Not a good match this year. Must stay aloof.
DRAGON with TIGER	A love hate relationship, more hate than love.
DRAGON with RABBIT	Environmentally friendly couple stay close
DRAGON with DRAGON	Heavy going and very competitive
DRAGON with SNAKE	A challenging year when neither has it easy
DRAGON with HORSE	Beneficial bonding goes beyond handholding
DRAGON with SHEEP	Misunderstandings cause tension
DRAGON with MONKEY	Allies stand in support of each other
DRAGON with ROOSTER	Benefiting hugely from Rooster's luck
DRAGON with DOG	Still a non-starter in the relationships stake
DRAGON with BOAR	A lacklustre relationship but restful

For the Dragon, this is a year when you could succumb to the temptation of being quite offhand with those who may not appear "your type". The Dragon can take a rather aloof view of the world and in 2012, they can blow hot and cold.

Your tolerance level is not high and you can get stressed out and easily aggravated. This is a shame because in 2012 you need the strength that others lend you as much as you need their goodwill. This is thus a year when it benefits the Dragon to put on a smiling face and to go out there into the world and make friends!

Do take note that your Life Force energy level is at an average level and your Chi Essence is low, so you will lack the inner strength to rise above aggravations and disappointments in relationships. And this is a year when you will get hurt by the presence of the five yellow affliction in your chart, something that causes obstacles to take you off course and cause you to be disappointed.

You will benefit very much if you take a more tolerant and positive attitude towards others in 2012, as this enables you to tap into the enhancing dimension of the year's energies. It is YOUR year, so do make a real effort to rise above frustrations and disappointments, to overcome your own natural snobbishness and off handedness with those who do not meet with your expectations. Instead try and reach out; you will find that friendships then become sweeter and happier. You might even find you rather enjoy being more sociable!

Basically according to the astrological sciences, how negatively or positively one reacts to or turns away in boredom from people depends very much on the "connection" one has with the other sign and how the energies of the year reacts with both signs.

People who let you down and how you respond to them also depends on who it is you are interacting with. The Dragon personality is usually not very mindful of other people's sensitivities; and you also do little to curb whatever impatience you may be experiencing at any time.

However, with certain animal signs, the Dragon will bend backwards to be accommodating. The Dragon is always able to turn on the charm when it wishes to, and indeed, that is when Dragon can be quite irresistible. In this, you are very much influenced by

129

how their astrological and chi energy reacts with you, and how they react with the energy of the year. Whether you feel well disposed to your friends and members of your family; whether you feel attraction towards new friends, seek out their company, get obsessed by sparks of "love" igniting or feel absolutely no affinity at all - your feelings and emotions, attitude and level of warmth sent outwards, all hinge on what we term the "relationship" luck you enjoy with them in any given year. And this changes from year to year.

Animal signs generally interact in a positive way toward their Zodiac allies, secret friends and astrological soulmates. But the extent of affinity does magnify or get reduced according to the feng shui energy of each sign in different years. So while it is absolutely important to know about these groupings, it is equally important to fine tune the level of affinity enjoyed each year.

Each sign also has another sign with whom it may be difficult to feel much warmth towards - we call the energy that flow between them arrows of antagonism. It can be troublesome when someone you care for, or have just met and feel attracted to, belongs to an

130

ARROWS OF ANTAGONISM

This diagram here shows the **arrows of antagonism** within the astrology wheel. It is possible for two animal signs who are "astrological enemies" to get along when both are going through good years, or when you both have strong inner chi essence in your annual chart.

animal sign that is supposed to be your astrological "enemy" - these are signs placed directly opposite you in the Astrology wheel. The good news here is that feelings of antipathy too can get reduced when both signs go through good years. Or when both have strong inner chi in their element chart.

Auspicious Crosses

Having said this, it is always to be preferred for siblings to be astrological allies, so planning your family this way has obvious benefits. But there is an astrological 'secret' that you can activate to create extremely strong lucky vibes for the entire family. This is referred to as the *Auspicious Crosses* formed by four members within a family unit. These crosses exist in a family when there are two specific pairs of antagonistic siblings.

The Earth Cross

For instance, families who have the Earth Cross comprising **a Dragon, Dog, Sheep and Ox** can create a very auspicious vortex of luck for the whole family. So, if in your family you have the antagonistic pair of Dragon and Dog, and you the Dragon are having issues with the Dog, then it is a great idea to try bring in the pair of animals that enable you to create the Earth Cross in your family. Here we are referring

THE EARTH CROSS

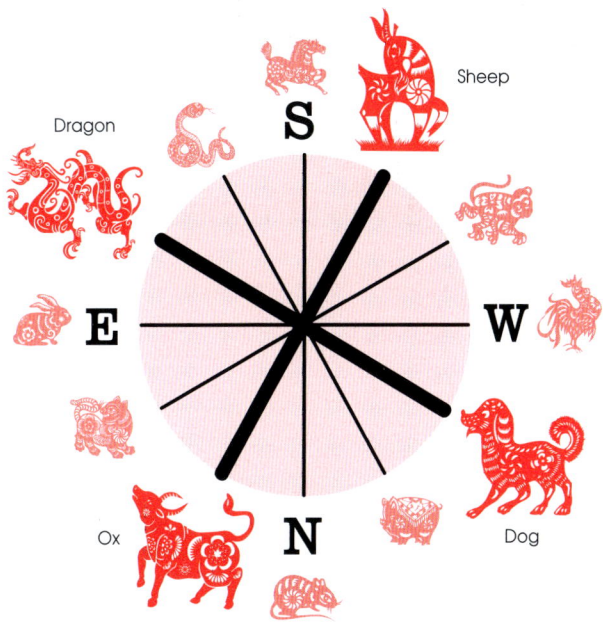

For the Dragon, if you are in a difficult relationship with a Dog person, bringing in a Sheep and an Ox into the fold can alleviate your problems and instead, turn your union into a very auspicious one indeed.

only to the basic family unit and it is necessary for all four signs to live in the same house. This is the Cross where all the animals belong to the Earth element. If you have this phenomena in your family already, then 2012 will be an amazingly prosperous year for you! This is because in 2012 the element of Earth stands for wealth luck and financial success.

The Thunderbolt Crosses

Another very auspicious combination is the Thunderbolt Cross. There are two such crosses and they are also created with two sets of animal signs, the first being the Dragon, Snake, Dog and Boar, and the second created by the Sheep , Monkey, Ox and Tiger.

These combinations create power and great influence within the family and at least one member of the family will become either very wealthy, or hold very high office in politics. Each of these combinations has two Earth signs.

It is important to understand that different years bring you different kinds of relationship luck. Remember that Dragon is definitely not in an enthusiastic mood in 2012, so the usually flamboyant and dynamic Dragon will be rather more low key this year. You are not in a mood to celebrate with friends

THUNDERBOLT CROSSES

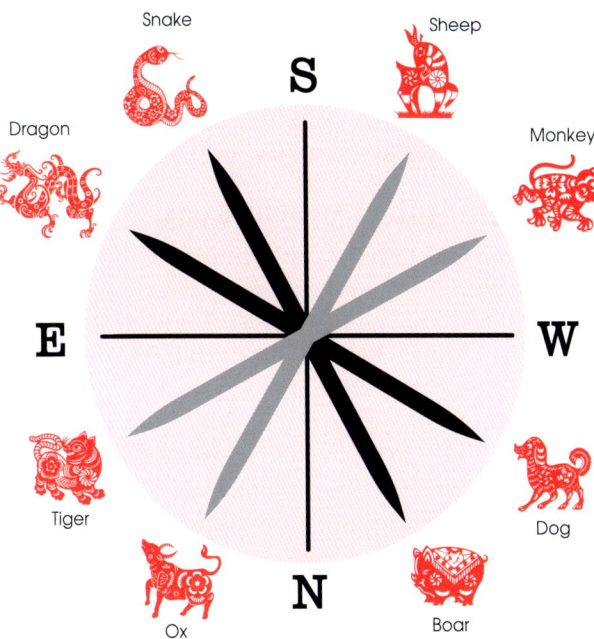

If all four animals of either of these Thunderbolt crosses, made up of animal signs in the secondary directions, live in the same house, this brings fabulous luck for each of them. The Snake, Dragon, Dog and Boar make up one Thunderbolt Cross. The Tiger, Ox, Sheep and Monkey make up the other.

or colleagues and those who wish to party with you must understand this. You are not being anti-social.

The Dragon's Allies

Your allies are the **Rat** and the **Monkey**. So these are the two signs you have great compatibility with, and your energy mixes well with theirs and vice versa.

As this is the Year of the Dragon, you are actually the flag bearer of the energy that pervades the year. The Dragon's luck however is afflicted by the five yellow & the Monkey's luck is hit by the number 3 quarrelsome star. And since the Rat is also afflicted by the illness star, it seems like all three of this trinity have quite a lot to cope with this year. This is thus not a strong trinity in 2012 and the main thing bonding this alliance is that it is the year of the Dragon! This year this trinity should stand close together!

The good news is that you will feel much closer to one another in 2012. This always happens when the feng shui winds of the year bring problems and afflictions to all three signs within any Triangle of Affinity. So in terms of compatibility, you get along really well with each other this year, lending strength, trust and friendship to one another.

FENG SHUI TIP: To harness maximum benefit from your affinity with each other, it is beneficial to carry the symbolic image of your allies. In 2012 the best for the Dragon born is to carry **the image of the high energy Monkey**, who is the bright spark of this trinity.

You can also wear your own sign of the Dragon as a ring or pendant - as a jewellery item, or you can display the Dragon image in your home. Inviting the image of the Dragon into your home will also bring the symbolic presence of this great celestial guardian close to you; this is sure to strengthen your life force and chi essence as well and hence would benefit you.

The Dragon and both its allies are known for their competitive spirit; these are action-oriented people who are incredibly mindful of making real progress in whatever they undertake. All three of the signs in your affinity triangle are self-motivated and can be highly disciplined attending to work; and also attending to your relationships. You will be "nice" to people you like and be very indifferent to those who you are not convinced can be "helpful" to you. Very calculating, but that is how you are. From this perspective, the Dragon can be very politically savvy…

Dragon, Rat and Monkey generally have a tendency to become very individualistic, and even quite opiniated. So relationships between these signs tend to be amiable but noisy. But all three of you are people with substance who have determination and perseverance.

You have the stamina to stay around for the long term, working at making your friendship, or work relationship or romance work. So for the Dragon to get into a relationship with another Dragon, with a Rat or with a Monkey, chances are that there will be good affinity flowing between you. The main problem for all three signs is that all of you have your luck afflicted in some way in 2012.

The **Dragon, Rat & Monkey** form an affinity triangle, thus there will always be good affinity flowing between you.

PAIRINGS OF
SECRET FRIENDS

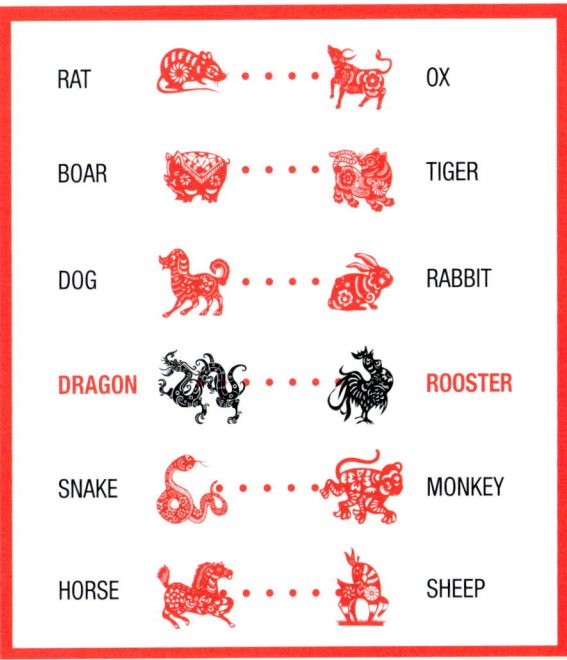

RAT		OX
BOAR		TIGER
DOG		RABBIT
DRAGON		**ROOSTER**
SNAKE		MONKEY
HORSE		SHEEP

Secret friends enjoy a very special relationship with
each other, and are able to help one another just by
associating with one another.

139

DRAGON WITH DRAGON

In 2012, heavy-going & very competitive

Two Dragons will either be great friends or bitter enemies. People born under this sign tend to be strong characters and unless the bond they can create with each other can override their naturally competitive nature, it is just a matter of time before they start to view each other with suspicion and distrust. But should they succeed in working effectively together, then it is likely one will have emerged as the de facto leader in the relationship. This then puts them naturally on the same side.

Dragons who are romantically involved with each other are likely to have carved out their respective spheres within the relationship, so one does not step on the toes of the other. The great thing about two Dragons is that they rarely vent their frustrations on those they love or with whom they are in some kind of partnership.

(*A Union with Potential* ★★★★)

More likely, there could develop a coolness should they disagree, so despite their fiercely strong personalities and stubborn attitudes, it is unlikely this couple will exchange strong words; but in a break-up, they are likely to become fierce adversaries.

When there is love factored into the equation however, they have the capability to transcend their differences and then this couple becomes quite formidable indeed. This is when it becomes two action-oriented people bringing out their best. They will achieve much when they working together towards the same goals, and the synergy generated then becomes both powerful and effective. Outsiders will find it hard to break through the partnership.

The Dragon personality is independent, so in a pairing of two of this sign, it is unlikely that either one will lose his or her identity. They will stay as two independents rather than merge into a single entity.

As professionals it is possible for them to carve out completely different and separate careers with both being successful. Will there be competition between them? Most certainly, but it will not be negative, because the Dragon possess the ability of respecting another who has the capability. Here the competition can be healthy and honourable.

DRAGON WITH RAT

In 2012, a great year to inspire each other

The Dragon and Rat have great affinity with each other. They gravitate to one another naturally and they will always take the other's side against all others; so this is a very loyal pair and they make great team mates or working colleagues; and usually they will develop a strong bond of friendship that lasts for a lifetime.

Theirs is a connection that is both special and unique as there is respect. There can be great affection as well. It is likely also for there to be a good deal of dry humour passing back and forth. In the crunch, these two signs stand up for one another.

All these positive traits get strengthened in 2012 and are very much in evidence. It is not surprising, because (with the Monkey) they make up the most strongly positive of the trinity of allies of the Zodiac. The Rat and Dragon will inspire each other in 2012 whether they are a romantic couple, business partners, siblings or professional associates. Their special affinity shines through and ensures that they see themselves through the year safely. Despite whatever setbacks or obstacles that may manifest for them individually or jointly, they will put up a united front.

But neither the Dragon nor the Rat are physically strong this year. Both can get hit by illness afflictions although at different times of the year. Illness can weaken resolve, but it is unlikely to weaken the spirit of either; the Rat is clever and the Dragon is courageous. Together, their spirit is strong, so as a couple or as partners, they will weather the year well.

The energy level generated by them together provides an excitement that drives boredom out the window. There will always be something for them to talk about or plunge into, and while 2012 is not a year when either is exactly brimming over with great ideas, nevertheless, Dragon's energy strongly dominates the year.

The Dragon and Rat make a fabulous pair.

And within the larger picture the world is going through a transformational time - something that really does catch the imagination of both the Rat and the Dragon. In 2012, their attention will be focused on making it through this bigger picture of a world in turmoil rather than on making big strides in their own personal material world. It is this ability to identify with each other on these same lines that they will bring out the best in each other.

Working and inspiring one another, they will channel their ambitious nature and strong personalities into some pretty worthwhile causes. The Rat has the capacity to be very creative in utilizing its talents. The Rat is also very strategic in thinking through whatever path it sets itself. What is great is that the Rat respects its Dragon partner or spouse as being something of a visionary, so together this pair can most definitely make 2012 a very exciting time indeed.

FENG SHUI ADVICE: Both of you should definitely bring the image or **images of the Dragon** into the home. The energy exuded by the Dragon benefits the Rat very substantially. Capture the chi essence of the year and it is sure to benefit the overall relationship between this pair.

144

Both Dragon and Rat should bring an image or images of the Dragon into the home this year. This will benefit you both greatly.

DRAGON WITH MONKEY

In 2012, these allies stand in support of each other

The Monkey is the other ally of the Dragon and this too is a pairing that is quite a superb fit. The Dragon can attain great heights with the Monkey by its side, especially in 2012 when those born under the Monkey sign are feeling rejuvenated and a lot stronger. Despite it falling under the influence of the number 3 star making it more impatient and belligerent than usual, the Monkey is a potentially a key asset to the Dragon.

Indeed, in 2012, this is quite an extraordinary pairing. The Monkey is probably the one sign that can galvanize the Dragon's energy levels and get Dragon enthused and excited. These two signs make excellent soulmates because Monkey's strategic and cunning mind finds such amazing resonance with Dragon, and this being its own year the energies will favour them.

In a love relationship between this pair, a great deal of mutual benefit gets created. Here, similar aspirations and similar outlook on life brings about harmonious communication and the Monkey demonstrates greater patience and goodwill than it would with others. The relationship between them is thus likely to be very satisfying.

(*Attaining Great Heights Together* ★★★★★)

In 2012 Dragon and Monkey will be flying high together, although career-wise, Monkey will tend to fly higher! This could instigate jealousy in the Dragon and that is the main thing to worry about in this pair's relationship. Sure they will stand together against others, but should they be pitted against one another in competition or find themselves in such a situation, Monkey's hostility could well over!

The charts show uneven luck for them both and Dragon especially has a lot on its plate this year, so working as a team could well be rather challenging but this is a pair that can create good synergy, so it benefits Dragon to take a humble posture in 2012 and go with the year's flow of energies. Romantically and in any professional partnership, you can both generate some incredible energy, so combining forces and skills to work towards a shared goal is the best way to go. It is also the way forward to cementing a really good relationship.

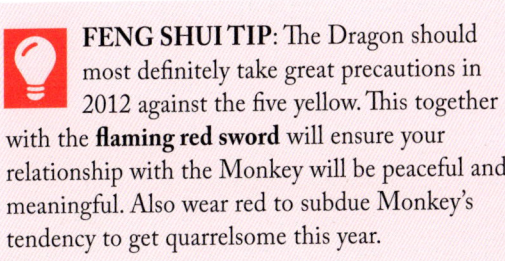

FENG SHUI TIP: The Dragon should most definitely take great precautions in 2012 against the five yellow. This together with the **flaming red sword** will ensure your relationship with the Monkey will be peaceful and meaningful. Also wear red to subdue Monkey's tendency to get quarrelsome this year.

The Dragon's Secret Friend & Zodiac Housemate

In addition to astrological allies, the Dragon also has a Secret Friend and a Zodiac Pal with whom it creates an incredibly special relationshi,; one that is even more influential than anything developed with one of its two allies.

The Dragon's secret friend is the Rooster, and together they signify the coming together of the heavenly pair the celestial Dragon and Phoenix, who together symbolize the best of a love or marriage relationship.

Secret friends are exceptionally compatible and should they marry, they create a powerful alliance that can weather any kind of bumps and difficulties. This is a pair that will stick together through thick and thin despite whatever problems or difficulties that may confront them. They bring amazing good luck to each other, and in 2012, the Dragon will be aided very significantly by the Rooster!

THE 6 DIFFERENT ZODIAC
HOUSE PAIRINGS

ANIMALS	YIN/YANG	ZODIAC HOUSE	TARGET UNLEASHED
RAT	YANG	HOUSE OF CREATIVITY & CLEVERNESS	The Rat initiates
OX	YIN		The Ox completes
TIGER	YANG	HOUSE OF GROWTH & DEVELOPMENT	The Tiger employs force
RABBIT	YIN		The Rabbit uses diplomacy
DRAGON	YANG	HOUSE OF MAGIC & SPIRITUALITY	The Dragon creates magic
SNAKE	YIN		The Snake creates mystery
HORSE	YANG	HOUSE OF PASSION & SEXUALITY	The Horse embodies male energy
SHEEP	YIN		The Sheep is the female energy
MONKEY	YANG	HOUSE OF CAREER & COMMERCE	The Monkey creates strategy
ROOSTER	YIN		The Rooster gets things moving
DOG	YANG	HOUSE OF DOMESTICITY	The Dog works to provide
BOAR	YIN		The Boar enjoys what is created

DRAGON WITH ROOSTER

Benefitting hugely from Rooster's Luck

The Dragon's relationship with the Rooster is really special, and more so than ever in 2012 when it is the Dragon who needs the Rooster 's luck more than ever.

In this pairing, either side can be play the role of the hidden mentor or the invisible supporter to the other, and because of the way the energy of the year is working out, it does appear that 2012 will be rather special for this pair; with the Dragon supplying the power of its intrinsic energy and the Rooster calling on an especially set of element energies as well as being helped by fabulous feng shui winds.

In any year, the Dragon gives amazing support to the Rooster and vice versa. This reflects the Rooster's celestial alter ego, the Phoenix, so Dragon and Rooster together is like the celestial pairing of the Dragon and Phoenix, destined to become soulmates and helpful allies.

(*Smitten With Each Other* ★★★★★)

Should they marry, they have the good karma to look forward to a happy and fruitful life together. There is fabulous luck in store for the Rooster in 2012 and a great deal of this will ripen on the Dragon should they do things together.

The beauty in this relationship is that both are such self-sufficient and independent individuals, capable of doing just as well on their own. Yet they can also live amicably together and bring special synergistic advantages to one another within a business partnership. In fact, should this pair marry, it is likely they will work together and also have their own separate projects that are independent of theother.

Dragon benefits from capturing Rooster's competence and expertise, while Rooster appreciates Dragon's far-sighted vision, zeal and enthusiasm. As such, each will forgive the other's occasional showy arrogance. In fact, Dragon is usually so smitten that Rooster's tendency to strut around being bossy and domineering will be overlooked. In later years of course, this can become a problem but even then, the extraordinary connection between these two signs can overcome almost anything.

Dragon and Rooster give power to each other, fuelling both the material as well as the spiritual dimensions of their lives. In 2012, Dragon benefits from the sheer strength of Rooster's fortitude and inner essence. The Rooster enjoys the OOO ranking in Spirit Essence in the Element chart, and as if that were not enough, the Rooster also enjoys the OOO in his/her Life Force as well as the Big 8 in the Flying Star chart. These indications bring enormous power to their chi energy in 2012.

 FENG SHUI ADVICE: To ensure great good luck, Dragons should bring **an image of the Rooster** into the home, either as a painting, a carving or as a **golden Nine Phoenix screen**. This harnesses the incredible synergy between these two signs.

A nine-Phoenix screen in the home will help create incredible synergy for a Rooster and Dragon pairing.

DRAGON WITH SNAKE
In 2012, a challenging year
when neither has it easy

The Dragon and Snake are two signs that create amazing magic together, and this should not surprise anyone, because this pair create what is known as the *House of Spirituality* together.

Indeed whatever, the circumstances or situation this is a couple who have eyes only for each other with the Dragon totally mesmerized by the Snake and the latter completely bowled over by the Dragon. The magic they create is something special only to them so that the house they build together shines brilliantly.

In 2012 however, a certain amount of fatigue enters the picture so that despite it being a Dragon Year, it is a time when the challenges facing both these two signs could cause them to become exhausted.

The Snake will feel the effect of a sudden lowering of Chi Essence, while both feel the fierce effect of the *five yellow,* that misfortune - bringing star. So there will be a great deal of challenges in 2012, not least of which will be ill health and all kinds of small and

153

big obstacles making life very aggravating indeed. The Snake of course is the charming and irresistible seductress of the Chinese Zodiac and the Dragon, its celestial lord. Together, these are the *Mystical Magicians* of the Cosmos and irrespective of what the year may bring, their allure for one another could well blind them to whatever challenges may confront them.

> Once ignited, the spark that gets lit between this pair could well make them blind to challenges and so they create magic by simply ignoring the bumps and the obstacles! This should not be surprising really, because together, the Snake and the Dragon become an indomitable pair with the extrovert Dragon playing the part of the **Magician** and the introvert Snake taking on the role of the **Mystic**. It is all rather esoteric as they explore the metaphysical world together.

Should they marry, the celestial or mysterious overtones of their relationship will develop slowly. But both are besotted with each other and the pairing works well. They can forge a long term relationship and create much happiness together. Their shared interests enable them to create a very private world which others cannot penetrate. What is amazing is that neither will cram the other's style.

These are highly individualistic signs, who could well enter into light and superficial relationships with others while still professing love for one another. Should there be any infidelities in this relationship, they will, surprisingly be able to live through the experience and even come out of it none the worse for wear. Their special kinship will ensure that for most of the time they have stability in their relationship.

The Dragon's Astrological Enemy

Astrological feng shui relating to relationships and compatibility between the twelve animal signs must also take note of one's "astrological enemy". This is represented by the animal sign that directly faces you on the Compass Wheel. In the case of the Dragon, your enemy is said to be the Dog, so between these two signs affinity cannot run deep.

As siblings, having a pair of astrological enemies in a family can be a problem, as there will always be latent hostility and tensions... unless of course there is also a Sheep and an Ox, in which case the family as a unit forms the Earth Cross of animal signs placed signifying the union of the 4 Earth element animal signs. Then, any animosity easily transforms into a very potent combination that not only get on well but also bring a great deal of power and auspiciousness.

PAIRINGS OF
ASTROLOGICAL ENEMIES

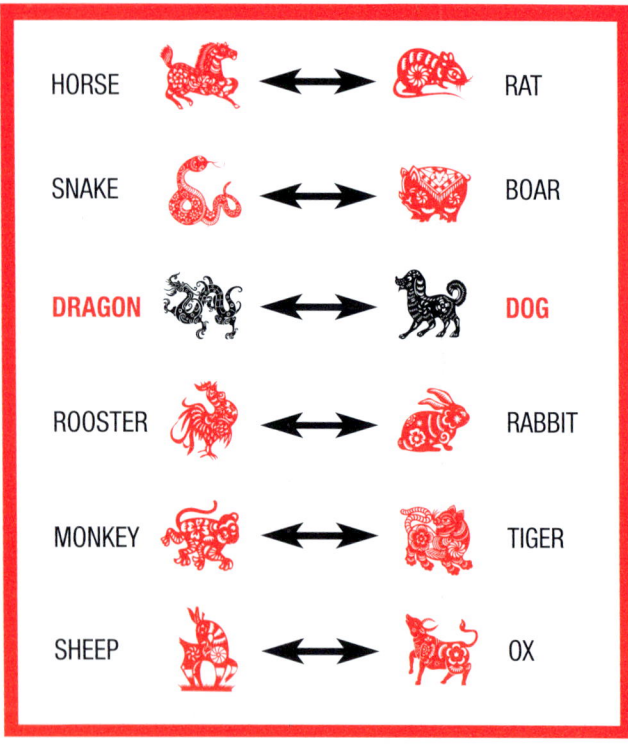

HORSE	⟷	RAT
SNAKE	⟷	BOAR
DRAGON	⟷	DOG
ROOSTER	⟷	RABBIT
MONKEY	⟷	TIGER
SHEEP	⟷	OX

It is difficult for a pair of astrological "enemies" to last together long term as a couple unless there is something else in the equation helping them.

In 2012 the Earth element signifies wealth and financial success, so any family having the Earth Cross phenomenon is likely to benefit significantly from the year's energy patterns.

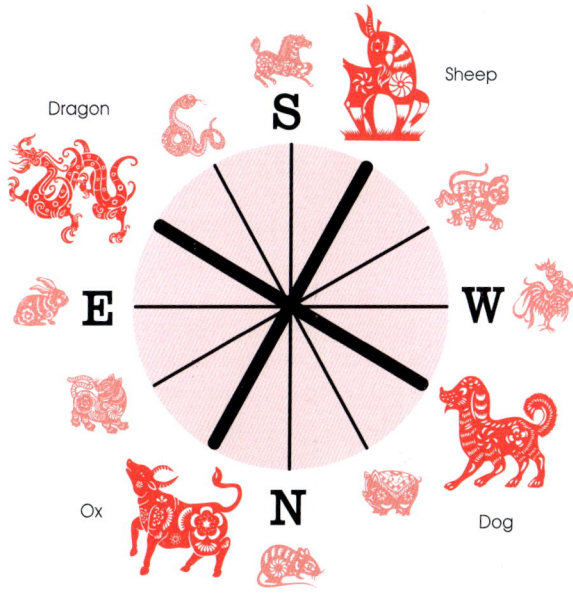

The Dragon born can benefit from the Earth Cross, made up of the Dragon, Dog, Ox and Sheep.

DRAGON WITH DOG

In 2012, still a non-starter in the relationships stakes

The Dragon and Dog are well known horoscope adversaries, but both are associated with auspicious Earth element, which in 2012 signifies prosperity and financial success. This may be good for them individually or under the circumstances of the Earth Cross combination, but because in the Astrological Compass Wheel they are located directly opposite each other, they tend to have a natural enmity to each other, much like the Ox and the Sheep, both also Earth signs of the Zodiac.

The four of these signs make up what is referred to as Earth Cross of the Compass. Separately the two sets are foes but if the four Earth animals can form a grouping they instantly create good fortune collectively.

But generally speaking and for most years, Dragon and Dog do not do much good for each other. They tend to bring out the worst in one another, find fault and generally cause negative instincts to surface. They can rarely work harmoniously together or live happily under the same roof, so for them to become a couple is generally not advisable.

In 2012, the Dragon can try to bring new energies to the Dragon/Dog relationship as it is the Dragon Year. But in the long run, this could well be just an exercise in futility.

This is because should they get together, the Dragon/Dog relationship is unlikely to last. There will be a superficiality in their relationship that does not bear going too deep. It is a shame, because separately, they will exhibit none of the negativities they manifest when they are a couple.

Each can be quite a star separately but brought together, should they spend enough time together, underlying differences are bound to surface and these get stronger and stronger until things explode. So this is not a union which has much chance of long term happiness.

However, should they have children that help them create the *Earth Cross* i.e. with two children born Ox and Sheep, then the foursome will generate good fortune together. So in terms of compatibility, on the surface, this is a pair that cannot tolerate each other easily.

DRAGON WITH OX

In 2012, not a good match. Must stay aloof.

These two are very powerful signs of the Chinese Zodiac and in 2012, it appears like they are simply going to overwhelm each other. So although this would normally be a good match, getting together or doing anything substantial together this year could well prove to be difficult.

Indeed, the advice is for the Dragon to leave the Ox behind, and for the Ox to stay aloof from the Dragon. Both sides should keep a distance from the other.

Ordinarily, the two of you are great for each other, one benefiting from the challenge of the other. You can even inspire and encourage one another to heights of excellence.

But in 2012, Dragon is weak while Ox is strong. And what's more, Dragon is afflicted. Thus these two have very unequal energy levels. So it is unlikely they can frolic as well as during years when the balance is not so out of sync.

The year thus does not favor this match too much. Better for both to stay a little aloof, each doing their own thing and carving out their own little space in the Universe; especially if you are already married or in a relationship. There is good long term affinity between the two of you - it's just that this is a year which can be too overwhelming for the Dragon, whose aura is afflicted, so it is better not to make out so much this year.

In 2012, the situation is fraught with the potential for disagreements, and uneasy egos can cause mistrust to dirty the scenario. Disagreements between strong signs often breed deep-seated hostility.

But both of you can take heart that between you in this relationship there is great underlying warmth. This is because the Dragon really is very simpatico with the Ox, and in a long-term relationship, neither sign has any intention of dominating the union.

If you can work together, you can achieve great things, especially when your energy patterns are in sync. That is when cooperation and goodwill flows easily, and when you can quite easily cooperate. But this can happen only when both your chi strengths are equal. The best way to deal with each other in 2012 is to give each other enough space for the Ox to build for the future and for the Dragon to cope with problems and to put out fires.

> For both Ox and Dragon, the year is a busy one filled with many distractions. There is also the challenge of living through rather turbulent times. This is not after all an ordinary year. The outlook is transformational and changes across an entire spectrum of disciplines are fast-moving as well as life changing and far reaching in their impact.

Against such a background, Dragon will find that Ox is not the best sort to get into bed with. Things simply get too complicated. Ultimately, it will be that there are more differences than similarities between you, so best to take a year off from each other!

The Ox and Dragon make a good match, but 2012 may be difficult.

DRAGON WITH RABBIT

In 2012, environmentally-friendly couple stay close

The Rabbit sign should enjoy frolicking with anyone born in the year of the Dragon and especially in a Dragon Year! This is a year which favors both these signs getting together, and although the Dragon has to put up with the *five yellow* afflictive star, nevertheless, getting together with Rabbit should strengthen Dragon's defences.

These two signs will enjoy building a love nest together simply because they have many things in common including their taste for luxurious things. This meeting of the minds creates a good foundation for them to get closer. Both signs are likely to be inspired by the latest trendy thing e.g. being ecologically friendly to the environment.

Their ability to work together on the same cause should also fan the relationship further in 2012. The good thing about a Rabbit pairing up with a Dragon will be the relative serenity of this couple. There will be few if any loud words between them, and even though the Dragon is a rather domineering kind of person, the Rabbit has no problem taking this in its stride. In fact, the Rabbit could find the Dragon's arrogance attractive. There is no problem here.

Nor will there be any seriously competitive vibes flowing between this pair. This is a very supportive relationship and there is little danger of either looking outside the relationship to assuage either their egos or their libidos.

This relationship does not get spoilt by petty egos clashing. The Rabbit has no problem creating a stable relationship with the Dragon as they are both able to see the big picture and instinctively work towards achieving results they both desire. This characteristic makes an excellent basis to create something potentially sound and lasting together.

This goodwill between the two signs arises from their connection to the season of Spring which forges a very special connectivity between these two signs. When it comes to forging a united front especially to deal with troublemakers or to withstand jealousy from outsiders attempting to upset their equilibrium, this pair has no difficulty in standing together.

Their loyalty to each other is stable, thus they create a very special resilience which creates a great deal of happiness for them. The Dragon can fly as high or as far as he/she wishes, and the Rabbit is always around to offer support and a helping hand.

The Dragon and Rabbit are loyal to one another and make a loving couple.

DRAGON WITH TIGER

In 2012, a love-hate relationship; more hate than love

This is a pairing of two powerful and strong personalities. The Dragon and Tiger have celestial auras and strong charismas! Should they forge a partnership together, respect is sure to flow easily between them; and if the truth be told, because these two are such powerful signs going into a powerful year, there is nothing they cannot achieve together. The Dragon comes into its own during its own year even though its energy levels are a bit frazzled!

Those born of these signs enjoy the special magic associated with the celestials of these strong creatures, who the Ancients say enjoy the "Power of the Gods", and what they attain is dependent only on the size of their dreams!

In business or in a romantic situation, the potential for attaining high levels of satisfaction together exists. How good the end result will be depends on their individual luck this year, and in 2012, the Tiger has better chi essence than the Dragon, but it is a Dragon Year, so both creatures are riding high.

(*Can Be Good Together* ★★★)

In fact, both signs appear in the year's paht chee and this indicates a time of change.

In 2012, the vitality of the Tiger is stronger, but the luck of the Dragon shines far brighter. It is a year when both must agree on who is boss from the start. The urge to dominate is intrinsic in both, so the earlier the dominance issue is settled, the better it is for their future together. This also settles the highly volatile nature of this relationship. For this to work then, a certain self discipline is definitely needed. Both Tiger and Dragon must be accommodating.

WHO IS STRONGER? Here we are dealing with strong personalities and between these two there is a continual flow of positive and negative vibes. It would be accurate to describe this as a love-hate relationship with more hate than love.

There are difficulties associated with keeping the luster burning brightly, to an extent that sometimes too much heat causes them to burn out and tire of each other. The danger in a Tiger/Dragon pairing is how long it can last. It takes a lot to sustain the passion and intensity of this relationship. There is a greater need to forgive indiscretions and overlook infidelities. Anyone stepping out of line can cause a strong reaction. These signs do not forgive easily.

But strength of will cuts both ways, so their high ideals and dreams of success and conquests can work in their favor. The Dragon and Tiger both have leadership skills, and both have the capability to create a resonance with those skills that inspire each other. That is when the two can become a formidable team.

The goal of high attainments and a yearning for excellence drive them to keep going from one new benchmark to the next. The year 2012 is an excellent year to join forces and build on dreams together if they can tilt the balance to generate more love than hate.

The Tiger and Dragon are two strong personalities that can work together if they try.

DRAGON WITH HORSE

In 2012 beneficial bonding goes beyond handholding

Should these two signs get together, they are in for a very interesting year, for the Dragon and the Horse have a mutually productive/exhaustive relationship which is both mesmerizing and draining at the same time.

The Dragon's relationship with the Horse is on balance a middling kind of pairing that has the potential to rise to great heights, and in 2012, the Horse will try to take them high high higher! This reflects the Horse's heightened horse power in 2012, a year when the urge to win and fly and soar and drive itself to excellence is at top gear.

The trouble is that the Dragon does not appear to be in the mood for too much scaling of heights. The Dragon simply lacks the life force, the energy and worse of all, it lacks the inner chi essence which this kind of fast living takes.

So in 2012 should you the Dragon want to bond with the Horse, note that it goes far beyond hand-holding! Getting into a love or business relationship with the Horse can well turn out to be a lot more than what you bargained for. There is excitement and there is victory, but there is also danger and the magnified affliction of the three killings. This is the year when the Horse lives dangerously, and for the Dragon, already afflicted by the five yellow, it would seem rather unwise to flirt with dangerous scenarios.

This coupling brings two very magnetic people together. This is a couple with fire and wind, speed and strength; strong clashes and equally powerful passion. There will not be any kind of animosity because both signs are so egoistic and neither feels any inferiority to the other. Here it is more of a situation where two dynamic free spirits learn to adjust and adapt.

Those able to transcend their differences in levels of strength and energy will have a thoroughly enjoyable and passionate love affair. Those who cannot maintain the pace or keep up could fall by the wayside. Should this pair marry, it must be a love match as anything arranged is doomed from the start. They are too headstrong to generate the required patience of living together unless they already know and care for each other.

The Horse sets a big store by love and loyalty, and the Horse also simply assumes that its mate will go with it to the ends of the world. The Dragon can also be sufficiently romantically inclined to get carried away by the passion of the moment, but in 2012, it is good to slow down and to think carefully before plunging into too many new adventures!

There is always plenty of excitement in a Horse and Dragon pairing.

DRAGON WITH SHEEP
In 2012, misunderstandings cause tensions

Oh dear, the year 2012 does not sit kindly on this pairing of Dragon and Sheep. It seems that both have an array of afflictions that could prove too much for them to cope with. The Dragon has more than its hands full coping with the *five yellow* which can be so challenging. And especially since 2012 is a year when it also has a low level of chi essence. This means the Dragon needs to borrow strength from others and certainly the Sheep cannot help much.

The Sheep has to cope with its yearly killing star energy brought by the 24 mountains compass AND take care of the hostile 3 star at the same time, so the Sheep has its hands full. To get together with the Dragon can be something of a challenge indeed, especially since this pair has little in common. Communication between them is almost nil, so it is something of strain for them.

(*An Uncomfortable Relationship* ★★)

It is not easy to list all the differences between them, as this list is both long and wide ranging. There are simply no sparks flying here and in fact this pairing is quite dull and hard to conceive of them being together and dating, let alone being in love. There is little on which they can build a future on together, and because neither is in any way astrologically beneficial to the other, it is hard to even imagine them coming together at all.

This is not to say that either Dragon or Sheep is boring - just that there is absolutely no chemistry between this pair. Marrying one another will be like walking the road to nowhere. Their styles differ, as do their aspirations and their values. They look at life and the world through different lenses, so this is very likely a most uncomfortable relationship.

Thankfully, the Dragon and Sheep are likely to react with the coolest detachment towards each other. There is unlikely to be any kind of attraction between the two unless they are thrown into a situation when coming together as a couple becomes inevitable. But even then, incompatibility is obvious and boredom sets in quickly. In some cases boredom can lead to animosity and even hostility.

Usually if these two signs get together and build a happy life together, it is because one of them has the other's ascendant, which means either the Dragon was born in the hours of the Sheep (1pm to 3 pm) or the Sheep was born in the hours of the Dragon (7 am to 9 am). The Hour of Birth does exert favourable influence, making an otherwise incompatible couple see something positive in each other.

Generally speaking however this is not a couple with much to build on. In 2012, any coming together of this pair will see regular disagreements between them. The Sheep will seem too quarrelsome by half. It is a very noisy pair indeed and much better if they split!

Hard to make the Dragon and Sheep pairing work as there is little chemistry.

DRAGON WITH BOAR
In 2012, a lacklustre relationship, but restful

This year, the Dragon could well benefit from Boar's intrinsically restful nature, even though this is a sign that generally does nothing very exciting for the Dragon. And vice versa. The Boar and Dragon will simply exhaust each other and also drag each other down because neither of them has good level of Life Force or Chi Essence in 2012.

This is an unlikely match who requires feng shui help during the Year of the Dragon to make sure that the afflictions of the year do not harm them.

The Dragon has to cope with the *five yellow*, while Boar has the *Violent Star 7* bringing betrayal and cheating luck - totally unpleasant scenarios. It is not surprising that they are going to irritate rather than inspire each other a great deal, the Dragon thundering its protests at the obstacles it has to contend with, and the Boar whining away at the unpleasantness of getting robbed. It does not help that this is a pair of signs whose communication is rarely on the same wavelength.

The Boar's attitude in 2012 tends to be negative and complaining most of the time. Truly, life around the Boar can be tedious and not something the intolerant Dragon can put up with at all. So the relationship is at best lackluster and at worst annoying.

But Boar's whining is harmless and if the Dragon can close his ears, the Boar can be a more restful presence than other more volatile signs. Nevertheless, unless a powerful cause bonds them, it is unlikely that the Dragon will respond positively to any of the Boar's overtures.

Sadly, the Boar secretly envies the Dragon's self possession, confidence and easy courage. So if it exists at all, this is a one-sided relationship as Boar tries to latch on to Dragon's spirited and high flying attitudes.

In 2012, the Boar's Life Force and Spirit Essence are at a very low level, so it is a situation where the Boar could get the Dragon into trouble. If they are married, they will need to take remedial actions together such as participating in some charitable project to overcome the danger to the Life Force of the Boar and wearing amulets to protect against being hit by some spirit harm.

The Dragon is also not enjoying great strength this year but it IS the Dragon Year and this lends some cosmic energy to this sign. Still, it is beneficial to conserve energy.

The Dragon and Boar make an average couple,
but this pairing can work with some feng shui help.

Chapter Five

ANALYZING DRAGON'S LUCK FOR EACH MONTH IN 2012

This won't be an easy year for the Dragon. The Five Yellow star has flown into your sector and you are likely to meet up with obstacles and aggravations. While it could prove a testing year, those of you who persevere through difficult times have every chance of success. You enjoy a star of Big Auspicious coming from the direction of the Rabbit, indicating that someone born in the year of the Rabbit could be very good for you, either directly or indirectly. It is important to stay positive, but at the same time protect yourself against the conflict stars that come your way. Keep the five element pagoda in the SE and try to carry one with you at all times. Not a year to take risks or make major changes in your life. But those of you who stay focused and positive will see your efforts paying off when you least expect it.

FIRST MONTH
February 4th - March 5th 2012

A MONTH OF ROMANTIC ENTANGLEMENTS

Socially you are in your element this month, and you enjoy the company of new friends and acquaintances, but this could also spell trouble for those of you who are married. There are many distractions and temptations of the romantic kind, and of the sort that could derail your marriage or current relationship. Don't let your head be turned by someone who has eyes for you. Whatever you start with someone outside the marriage will be short-lived and almost certain to cause trouble for you in the long run. As long as you keep your head about you, you can make good headway in terms of establishing new friendships and building on rapport with important clients; just be sure whatever you work on is non-romantic in nature.

WORK & CAREER - Power of Speech

A promising month for Dragons focusing on their careers. Use this month to cultivate relationships with co-workers and your superiors. You have the power of speech and you will find others particularly responsive

179

to your suggestions this month. Share your ideas, they will be well received. If you have the right attitude, you will be able to cover a lot of ground, building a solid foundation to work from for the coming year. A good time to pursue those who have the power to make a difference to your career. It will be your charm and self-assured nature that impress others this month, so work on these.

BUSINESS - Social Skills

Use your social skills to network with others. It is an excellent time to widen your circle, and opportunities come to those of you who look for them. But while it is exciting to explore new pastures, don't neglect your existing customer base. The best way to improve things on the business front is not to shy away from challenges. There will be many different demanding your attention right now, but as long as you can mentally welcome the challenge, you're perfectly capable of handling many different responsibilities. The more you take on, the more you'll realize how under-utilized you were before.

LOVE & RELATIONSHIPS - Temptations

A month filled with traps and temptations. Don't let yourself fall into an illicit relationship. You'll find it easy to start, but impossible to get out of. Those of you who are married are in much more danger of a romantic scandal than the single Dragon, but even the singles should beware. There is danger of peach blossom luck, which manifests in romantic love entanglements that can cause a lot of trouble. Work relationship and friendships on the other hand have every chance of blossoming, as long as you don't let things take a romantic turn. You're sociable, affable and terrific company, putting you first on every guest list. Enjoy the month but play it careful when it comes to matters of the heart.

Dragons are advised to carry the **amulet against third party interference** in your relationships this month. Particularly if you are in a happy marriage.

EDUCATION - Study Luck

A fabulous month for the young Dragon. You enjoy infinite study luck with the number 4 scholarly star making an appearance in your chart. Make best use of this lucky time by putting in extra effort in class. This is also a good time to get to know your teachers better. You enjoy good rapport with others this month, and your easy charm will endear you to many. So do use this opportunity to build on relationships that matter.

SECOND MONTH
March 6th - April 4th 2012

THIS WILL BE A DISAGREEABLE MONTH. DO MANAGE YOUR ANGER!

There is plenty of quarrelsome energy present this month, and a high propensity for the Dragon-born to fly off the handle at the smallest thing. Others would be wise to stay well out of your way this month. Don't let your sullen disposition drive others away, and do try to recognize when others are trying to do something nice for you. If you change your attitude, you'll enjoy yourself a lot more this month. For some of you, there is danger of lawsuits and trouble with the law. It is better to keep a low profile this month and avoid invoking the jealousy of others. Don't brag or blow your own trumpet too much. Disputes that occur this month have a tendency to become more serious, and you are likely to be at the losing end.

Display the Red Dragon with Sword in the Southeast sector to improve your luck and to control the difficult energies.

WORK & CAREER - Challenging

Working life presents many challenges this month and you have many deadlines to meet which could get you down. Don't let stress overcome you. Put yourself in the right frame of mind. If you need to take some time off, plan for it. A weekend away could be just what you need right now. But resist the temptation to feel sorry for yourself. When you adopt a weak disposition is when others can get the better of you. There may be adversaries at work competing with you for the boss' attention, and when the energies are low in your chart such as this month, it is easy for them to belittle what you do. Display your secret friend the Rooster on your work desk; this will improve friendship luck and attract you allies at work, something you need badly right now. It will also prevent you from being politicked out of favor.

BUSINESS - Stay in Line

There may be staff issues to deal with. Beware the disgruntled employee, for he or she can make life more difficult than you think. Focus attention on making sure everyone who works for you is happy. It may be necessary to dig beneath the surface to see what is really going on. As long as you make the effort to find out, you won't uncover anything that cannot be solved. You may find those in authority making life difficult for you. Avoid risking being penalized. If there are licenses or permits you need to apply for in your work, be sure you have them well in advance. Don't try to outsmart the law. Stepping out of line just a little could have you caught out, because that's the way the hand is dealt this month. Also not a good month for signing agreements of entering into new deals.

LOVE & RELATIONSHIPS - Quarrelsome

A difficult month when it comes to relationships, particularly new ones just starting to develop. There is too much quarrelsome energy in your chart, so anyone you are with will tend to find you more disagreeable. Not a promising month to make a good first impression on anyone. Married Dragons and those in steady relationships are equally affected by the hostile star. You could find yourself fighting with your partner for no particular reason. Avoid being petty or making a big deal over small things. The straw that breaks the camel's back is within arm's reach; make sure you don't use it. Enhance harmony luck in your marriage with **six smooth round crystal balls** in the center of your home.

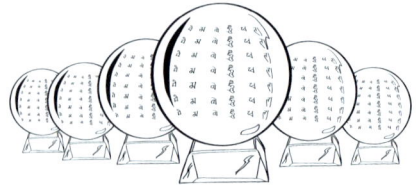

THIRD MONTH
April 5th - May 5th 2012

SERIOUS ILLNESS POSSIBLE. BE FUSSY ABOUT FOOD AND TEMPERATURES.

This is a month to be extra careful. The number 2 illness star has flown into your sector, combining with the annual five yellow in your chart. This indicates illness and risk of accidents. Try to lie low this month and avoid taking risks, especially physical ones. Those of you involved in dangerous sports should be more cautious this month. Do not drive too fast on the road, and plan ahead if you have to embark on long journeys. Be sure to carry the **anti-illness amulet** as this will help counter the unfortunate combination of stars in your chart this month. You can also carry the **Wu Lou**, also known as the health gourd; this is an effective cure for the illness star which gets magnified this month by the misfortune star. Elderly or sickly Dragons should avoid the Southeast sector this month. If your bedroom is located in the SE, it is worthwhile to move out for the month. Do watch what you eat, and if there is any indication of ill health, best to get checked out so you can nip whatever it is in the bud.

WORK & CAREER - Watch Your Back

This month your personal luck is very afflicted, making it difficult for you to excel. Trying too hard could make things worse. Try and take a relaxed attitude. Getting stressed out over small matters will only magnify them. Wear the color white, and also plenty of gold jewellery made into symbols of good fortune to counter the unlucky Earth element stars in your chart this month.

Don't expect to receive assistance from your colleagues or peers. Whatever you achieve will have to be achieved on your own this month. Also be careful whom you trust; even those you consider friends could betray your trust, sometimes unintentionally. Watch out for troublemakers and protect your back. Don't leave yourself open for criticism. Play your cards close to your chest. If you have any good ideas to share, best to wait till next month to share them if you want them well received.

BUSINESS - Maintain Status Quo

You don't have much luck in business this month, so it is better to maintain the status quo than to make any changes that are too drastic. Be careful when pursuing new strategies, especially those that open yourself up to risk. Financial luck is poor, so avoid investing big or taking a gamble. Watch your cash flow more closely and do not incur too many unnecessary expeditures. This is a time when it is better to conserve for the future. Competition from rival firms could heat up, seeing your market share quickly eroded. Preempt this by planning in advance. Be defensive in your strategies. Schedule important meetings and discussions for next month instead.

LOVE & RELATIONSHIPS - Sharing

Relationship luck is a lot better than your luck elsewhere this month. You will find your other half a great source of support during difficult and trying times. Sharing your problems with your spouse or partner is bound to relieve some of it, so open yourself up to him or her. For those whose marriage has suffered the trials and tribulations of many years together, this is the perfect opportunity to improve things between the two of you.

For the single Dragon, pursuing a love interest will take your mind off the less pleasant things in your life right now, which can only be a good thing. If you can adopt a more positive attitude and a less edgy disposition, the month is likely to roll along more smoothly for you.

FORTH MONTH
May 6th - June 5th 2012

SMALL SUCCESSES THIS MONTH BRING A BREAKTHROUGH

A much better month for the Dragon! This month is about new beginnings and starting afresh. Whatever wasn't working in your life before gets resolved. You will find things proceeding more smoothly and there will be fewer obstacles in your path to whatever you are hoping to achieve. Projects finally get completed and your professional relationships improve. You can expect some significant turning points in your life this month. Be prepared to undergo a process of change. It may be in your work or personal life, or even in the way you look at things. Whatever change comes will be positive, so there is no need to worry. Sometimes even if things develop in a manner you're not entirely happy with, trust that things will work themselves out by month end. Go with the flow.

WORK & CAREER - Pleasantly Fast-paced

You're in for a busy time at work. When you've completed one task, another gets set. There is plenty going on at any one time, but you'll find yourself thriving on the fast pace that this month brings.

A series of small successes at work culminates in a breakthrough, and there could be a cause to celebrate before the month is up. You have enormous drive this month, as well as good leadership charisma. You exude a confidence that reassures others. A great time to impress the boss and those who matter. Be prepared to showcase your talent. The Dragon is a naturally bragging type of personality, but if you do it with your innate charm, others will find it hard not to be impressed!

BUSINESS - A Transformational Time

A transformational time for Dragons in business. You can achieve a lot this month if you can accept, embrace and even foster change. Sure you can maintain the parts of your business that are doing well, but if there is a way to do things better, don't be stubborn to change. Productivity can increase manifold if you can be less inflexible. Getting used to a new way of doing things and a new style of working could prove tough for some of you, particularly to the older Dragons who are more set in your ways; but once you welcome the change that is taking place around you, you'll find yourself energized and revved up. Let your Dragon nature come forth. Don't dismiss any new or revolutionary ideas until you've given them a hearing.

LOVE & RELATIONSHIPS - Playing It Cool

This month favors your professional life more than your love life, unless you do not work. You're too busy chasing your career to put too much emphasis on romance at this time, and simply because there is so much going on that's exciting. This air of disinterest could actually be very promising for the single Dragon looking for a mate. The less interested you are, and the less available you seem, the more others will want you. Your focus will return to matters of the heart next month, so don't shut the door on any opportunity. But the advice is, playing it cool is definitely the right way to go for now!

EDUCATION - Victory Luck

The young Dragon has victory luck on their side this month! Enhance by carrying or wearing the **Victory Banner.** Those of you sitting exams can expect to do well as long as you're sufficiently well prepared. This is a good time to take up something new. The more you have on your plate, the better you will do. You are hungry for knowledge but sometimes need someone or something to motivate you to get started. You will also find a study-buddy a good idea; but for this you need another very like-minded student, else you will end up arguing and debating rather than getting any real learning done.

FIFTH MONTH
June 6th - July 6th 2012

OH DEAR, MISFORTUNE LUCK GETS STRENGTHENED

The magnifying star makes an appearance, multiplying the effect of the unfortunate five yellow in your chart. This brings hidden dangers this month, so do not let your guard down just because things were smooth sailing the month just passed. You can expect to meet up with obstacles and glitches in the course of your daily life, and some of these could be quite aggravating indeed. On the other hand, you could take these difficulties as the perfect learning opportunity. Nevertheless, it is also advisable to wear the necessary protection against afflicted stars, and the best for the Dragon this month is the **five-element pagoda**. Wear as a pendant or carry as a keychain.

WORK & CAREER - Believe in Yourself

Your luck is down and your confidence could have taken a recent hit. Don't rely on the opinions of others too much. Believe in yourself and stand firm when it comes to ideals. There could be temptations to bend the rules in exchange for favors, but straying from the path of righteousness will only get you into trouble.

191

Surround yourself with people who make you feel good about yourself, and if you cannot get that from your colleagues at work, lean on those who have your best interests at heart at home. Read the nuances in situations and don't offer your opinions nonchalantly. Everything you do and say will have an impact, and this month it is better to stay low key than to expose yourself to criticism.

BUSINESS - Maintain Your Morality

Business luck is not too promising this month, but be cautious when it comes to change. When things are not going right, it is natural to want to see what can be altered for the better. But when switching direction, just be sure you are not jumping from the frying pan into the fire.

It may be tempting to take on opportunities that allow you to make progress for the good of the business, sometimes at the expense of others. But maintain your morality as a major factor when making such decisions, because what you do now is almost certain to come back to haunt you later. It is better to hold back a little now. You may have to live through a rough patch, but things are sure to improve when the prosperity star pays a visit next month.

LOVE & RELATIONSHIPS - Love & Trust

You enjoy luck in relationships this month. Existing friendships have a particularly trusting quality about them that will help you through difficult moments in your life. One of these platonic friendships could well develop into something more if you let it happen. Those of you looking for love should open up your heart. Love does not always come as a bolt of lightning, and this month it could well blossom from a bud that was always there but unnoticed till now. Those of you who are married will see an improved closeness between you and your spouse. Conversation is important for bonding, and this means real discourse over real topics. But remember, if you want your partner to listen, making it a point to listen to them first will start the ball rolling in the right direction.

EDUCATION - Stamp Out the Stress

Try not to take on too much this month. Keep working conscientiously, but if you have too much to cope with, do remember to take a break. Don't let yourself get overly stressed out. Remember that there are always solutions to problems. And instead of trying to cope with stress all on your own, do share whatever is on your mind with those close to you such as your family. A burden shared is a burden lifted.

SIXTH MONTH
July 7th - Aug 7th 2012

EXCELLENT INDICATIONS OF A STRONG COME BACK FOR YOU THIS MONTH

This is an auspicious month when the number 8 wealth star flies into your chart. You can be sure that whatever you start this month has every chance of success. Do make the most of this fruitful time by taking on new challenges and being proactive when it comes to living. Work and business luck look extremely promising, and there are some truly exciting new ventures on the horizon. On the personal front, your life is sprinkled with a great deal of love and affection. This applies equally to married as well as single Dragons. A lucky time to propose marriage, get engaged, have a wedding. Any happiness occasion celebrated with a big party will serve to enhance your good luck further.

WORK & CAREER - A Promising Time

Things look very good for the Dragon when it comes to career matters. There is an atmosphere of trust and respect between yourself and your peers, and some exciting new projects to sink your teeth into.

Camaraderie among your colleagues gets improved and the backdrop at work changes from a competitive one to one of solidarity among team players. While this is a tempting time to push yourself forward and to showcase your skills, try not to do so at the expense of others, or you could make yourself some enemies you don't need. The Dragon who can be a real team player will be the one who excels this month. Take a step back every now and again to see the big picture. Those of you who have a macro view of the things you are working on will fare better than those that get too bogged down with details.

BUSINESS - New Opportunities

Those of you in business will benefit from having clearly defined objectives this month. Develop a strategy and build on it but do not get bogged down with details. Many new opportunities will be presenting themselves. Be courageous when venturing into new areas. You can afford to take some risks but having said that, because your life force and chi essence are not terribly strong this year, do not take uncalculated risks. If however things make sense, do not be afraid to go for it. When making any changes, do be sure all of the team knows about it. If you build on a concerted team effort, there is nothing that cannot be achieved by the Dragon-led venture this month.

LOVE & RELATIONSHIPS - Sociable

This is an uplifting month when it comes to love and relationships. You are feeling composed and contented, with a lot of loving from your other half. Your professional life is going well, leaving you more time to indulge in matters of the heart. Your happy-go-lucky attitude and great sense of humor are a huge hit among friends, and will win you lots of points with your partner as well.

This is a time to enjoy yourself, attend parties, and be as outgoing as you want. Nothing you say is in danger of being taken the wrong way, so you can be yourself and not worry about holding back. The positive energy you radiate makes this a good time to make new friends. Widening your circle of contacts will not only improve your social life, it will also bring you new opportunities in work and business.

EDUCATION - Believe In Yourself

There are many honors to win this month and you have everything it takes to make a good impression. This is the time for the young student Dragon to shine! Believe in your own abilities and there's nothing you cannot achieve. Don't be afraid to set the bar high, because the higher you aim, the better the results you can achieve.

SEVENTH MONTH
Aug 8th - Sept 7th 2012

PETTY BICKERING & SMALL DISHONESTIES EXHAUST YOU

A disagreeable month looms ahead with threat of petty bickering and small dishonesties. In more serious form, the danger to the Dragon could manifest as robbery or violence, so it is important to take personal security and safety seriously. Lady Dragons who stay out late at night should carry the **Nightspot Amulet** or suitable mantra protection, and if possible, have a chaperone or companion. Not a good idea to party too hard this month. Always keep your wits about you because you don't know who is trustworthy and who is not. You could find yourself cheated or betrayed even by those you trust, so watch your back. There may be some difficult challenges to grapple with, but nothing you cannot cope with if you face the problem head on. Give as good as you get if someone is being difficult, but fight with your brains not your brawn.

WORK & CAREER - Some Unpleasantness

At work you could experience a critical situation, but try not to blow anything out of proportion. Reacting calmly to any unpleasantness is the best move. If there is someone challenging you for your position or trying to undermine you to the boss, shrug them off and stand firm. If you are too weak to fight, their offensiveness will feed itself. Be prepared for some wolves in sheep's clothing, even among "friends". Carry the **Medallion for Protection against Third party Interference** to shield yourself against the worst of it, and maintain belief in your own abilities. As long as you are continuing to put in good effort at work, you have nothing to fear. Things may be difficult now, but will improve significantly by next month, when the heaven star pays a visit.

BUSINESS - Poor Judgment

With the robbery star hovering over your chart, there is risk of being swindled. Don't leave financial planning and monitoring to somebody else. If it is your own business, make it a point to be very hands-on, especially now when the stars indicate something amiss. In new ventures, make sure you have a water-tight agreement binding by law. It is better to spell things out clearly on paper, else a dispute could well arise, and sooner rather than later. It is probably not a good idea to enter into new partnerships right now; making a poor judgment is a real possibility when your luck is afflicted. Wait till better luck manifests for you before taking any risks with new endeavors.

LOVE & RELATIONSHIPS - Trust Needed

There may be trouble brewing when it comes to your love life. Arguments stemming from mistrust put a dampener on your relationships. It is important for both sides to trust each other, otherwise fear of infidelity from the other side could make either of you veer off the path or succumb to the advance of outsiders. Do not let yourself be influenced by others against your own partner. If you want your relationship to work, you may need to be more protective of your relationship than you currently are. Stand up for each other instead of allowing someone on the outside dictate how you feel.

EDUCATION - Fine Rewards

Effort put into your studies reaps fine rewards so it is worthwhile to put in the effort. Your strength of purpose and your ability to get what you want is stronger than usual, making it easy to forge ahead. Use this time to leapfrog your classmates and to take top spot if you so wish. Study luck is with you, and the more single-purposed you are, the better you will do.

EIGHTH MONTH
Sept 8th - Oct 7th 2012

A MONTH OF UNEXPECTED BREAKTHROUGHS - VERY LUCKY

This is a fine time for the Dragon with many unexpected breakthroughs! You are blessed with heaven energy, and opportunity after opportunity falls into your lap. You also have the luck of helpful people on your side, so if you need a favor or a helping hand, don't hesitate to pick up the phone to ask. When opportunities present themselves, be sure to move quickly to benefit from them. Maintain a sense of urgency when following up on leads, and let your instincts guide you. Be bold when making your move. There is little that will go wrong in your life right now, so you can be brave about your decisions.

WORK & CAREER - A Time to Impress!

Career luck is with you and chances are you already know exactly what you want to achieve. Your involvement with others is on extremely secure footing, and there are some helpful new influences available to you as mentor figures, to whom you can turn to for good advice. You pick up the pace this month, and delivering more than expected becomes the norm. This is a time when you can seriously impress as long as you don't lose focus. When it comes to your colleagues, be upfront and honest with them. Don't go behind their backs. It is easier to make it up the career ladder if you have the support of your co-workers as well as your superiors.

BUSINESS - Change of Pace

This is a time to look ahead. Your mind is extremely alert right now, allowing you to formulate clear and workable strategies from scratch. There is a definite change of pace and attitude from last month, making this a much more enjoyable and fulfilling time for the Dragon in business. Pet projects have a chance to take off, and if you need help for people holding positions of power, help presents itself, either through a friend, relative or chance meeting. Although it is not always wise to act on impulse, this is one of those times when you can trust your instincts a little more and go on feel rather than on analysis. Don't let good opportunities pass you by. This is a dynamic time for the Dragon, and could well be the time when you get your big break.

LOVE & RELATIONSHIPS - Quite Magical

This month will have an extremely positive effect on your love life. You have terrific magnetism which draws others towards you. Making conversation comes so easily to you, allowing you to build an instant rapport with whomever you meet. As well as making it easier for you to land yourself a partner, it also opens up your choices to suitable ones. You're less picky over the minor details that in the long run shouldn't matter, and this gives you access to some real gems you'd normally have missed.

Take advantage of the fact that you are lucky in love, and let the hand of fate take you where it will. If a spark of magic ignites, don't fight it. You have a lot to look forward to when it comes to romance and love this month. Dragons who are married also have a most enjoyable time ahead. Take this opportunity to resolve any differences you've had with your partner to build on a stronger union for the future.

EDUCATION - Anything is Possible

Your luck is very positive this month, and help is there if you need it. But more important than help and encouragement from others is your belief in yourself. If a voice inside you says you can't do something, do it anyway, and the voice will be silenced. Everything is possible when luck and good fortune shines down on you like it does now. Enjoy the month and use the positive energy to your advantage.

NINTH MONTH
Oct 8th - Nov 6th 2012

MONTH OF THE DOUBLING EFFECT; FOR YOU, A DOUBLING OF FIVE YELLOW.

The annual and monthly flying stars coincide this month, doubling any good or bad luck indications. Unfortunately for the Dragon, this means a magnification of the misfortune star number 5. Make sure you stay protected against this affliction by ensuring you have your cures in place. The best cure for the five yellow is the five element pagoda. Place a large enough one filled with earth from your garden in the Southeast part of your home. It is also a good idea to wear one as a personal protection amulet. Do not take risks this month. This is also the absolute wrong time to embark on new ventures or to make any major changes in your life. Avoid dwellings that are too yin in nature such as hospitals, cemeteries or prisons. Could be a good time to go away on holiday and not embark on anything or too much significance to your life right now.

It is important to suppress the double Five Yellow with a large enough 5 element pagoda this month.

WORK & CAREER - Troublemakers at Work

You may be feeling a little insecure, but don't let a lack of confidence be your downfall. Although you may have to cope with troublemakers trying to sabotage you, resist the temptation to retaliate without considering your position carefully first. It is never a good idea to take others on when you are down on your luck; you will almost certainly be on the losing end. If you find yourself in an unpleasant situation, concede defeat and save yourself for another day. It is wise to arm yourself with a Fire Totem talisman to protect yourself against coming to harm at the hands of a jealous competitor.

BUSINESS - Strong Competition

In business, things may not go as smoothly as you'd like, and likely there are battles to fight. Be prepared for some fierce competition from business rivals, but don't stoop to dirty tactics to get ahead. Those who outsmart the competition with clever tactics will do better than those who employ unjust methods. Be warned however that your luck is not at its best right now, and on the contrary, really quite poorly. It may be a better strategy to leave fighting back till next month when your luck improves. You will also enjoy more support from allies then. For now, maintain a low profile and try not to stir things up too much.

LOVE & RELATIONSHIPS - Emotional

Your feelings are much harder to control than usual, and if you are a naturally emotional person, this could make you quite difficult to deal with this month. When faced with any emotional situation, try to maintain a calm composure and always think things through before you act. Your reactions tend to be impulsive and not reflective of what you really want. Slow your brainwaves down when faced with a highly charged situation. This month it is better to focus on other areas of your life.

The single Dragon looking for love will not be as lucky as usual. Don't put your heart on the line or you may well have it broken, or bruised. For the married Dragon, avoid picking fights with your spouse for no reason. Home life would be so much more harmonious if you are willing to back down and give in once in a while.

EDUCATION - Confide in a Friend

An argument with a friend, problems at home or a personal crisis may be affecting your schoolwork. If there's something bothering you, try talking to someone about it. Remember that you don't always have to shoulder problems on your own. Talking to someone will almost always make things better.

TENTH MONTH
Nov 7th - Dec 6th 2012

DOMESTIC & PERSONAL MATTERS DOMINATE YOUR LIFE THIS MONTH

Your luck improves from last month and you're likely to feel a wave of relief. Obstacles that stood in your path before evaporate or at least get knocked down in size, and there is light at the end of the tunnel. Home issues and matters of the heart take center stage this month and there is much joy when it comes to your love life. Your social life heats up and friends become more attentive. You have an undeniable charm that draws others towards you and even those who previously had hostile feelings towards you react positively to you now. This is an ideal time to mend friendships and to get over old grudges. Work life gets enhanced by your ability to get along well with others. The nicer you are, the more you'll find others wanting to help you. Accept help offered graciously and you'll start to realize how much more pleasant it is working with others than against them.

WORK & CAREER - Stay Confident

Use this month to build friendships with those you work with. Your colleagues will be particularly responsive to your suggestions right now. Share your ideas with the intention of not just profiting yourself but working as a team. If you have the right attitude, you can cover a lot of ground building a solid foundation for the coming months. You have a newfound confidence that can be put to good use at the workplace. Use your natural leadership qualities to start new initiatives. If you maintain your belief in yourself, you will find things falling into place of their own accord. But above all, do not let yourself be easily swayed by others. Go with your instincts. As long as you don't let your confidence get rocked, there is nothing you cannot achieve right now.

BUSINESS - Effective Leadership

You are in a terrific position to achieve what you want if you stay organized and determined. Put your social skills to good use by careful networking. While your gregarious personality is a magnet for admirers, watch you don't start stepping on people's toes for comical effect. No one likes being the brunt of a joke no matter how innocent the motive, so don't go down that road. You have the ability to make people listen right now, so make what you say count. This is a brilliant time to motivate the staff and to galvanize the team. Direct more effort in this direction and you will see productivity at work increase manifold.

You make a good boss as long as you maintain clear objectives.

LOVE & RELATIONSHIPS - Passionate

Relationships started this month have every chance of success. You are in the mood for love and your enthusiasm rubs off on whoever you come into contact with. There will be many different possibilities suggesting themselves to you, but if you want to go beyond casual dating, try to stay monogamous. Juggling love interests will cause you more headaches than anything, and what starts out fun will turn into a living nightmare. Married Dragons or those of you already committed may find yourself attracted to someone outside of your current relationship. Beware such feelings unless you want to get yourself in trouble. If you star something outside the marriage, it will be you who gets hurt in the end. Wear or carry the **anti-infidelity amulet** this month to keep the peach blossom vibes in check.

EDUCATION - Fabulous Study Luck

An awesome time awaits the Dragon student thirsty for knowledge. You have the benefit of the scholastic star, which boosts your propensity to learn and also your success in examinations. Enjoy the good stars in your chart this month.

ELEVENTH MONTH
Dec 7th - Jan 5th 2013

NOT A GREAT MONTH AS THE BICKERING STAR CAUSES TEMPERS TO FLARE

Not the most agreeable of months as you have the quarrelsome star 3 in your chart. This makes you more irritable than usual, and unable to suffer fools at all. And while this is so, what makes you less of a fool than others? Try to be more agreeable if you want to keep your friends. One outburst too many and you could find others actively avoiding you. On a more serious note, lawsuits and legal entanglements are a real danger, and could afflict even the most unlikely of you. Beware also when dealing with the authorities such as the police or lawmakers of the land. Getting into a dispute with the law could cause you to lose more than you bargained for. Stay quiet and work on calming the mind. Display **Ksiddigarbha's Fireball** in the Southeast corner of the home and of the room where you work or spend the most time. This will help quell the hostile energies.

Ksiddigarbha's Fireball will help control the quarrelsome energies of the month.

209

WORK & CAREER - Disagreeable

The coming month will tend to be characterized by discontentment at work, with difficult relationships between you and your co-workers. Those of you Dragons who have to work in team situations with extensive contact and discussion with others could find the next few weeks very trying. Try to be more agreeable and to keep your temper in check. You're moodier than usual and shouldn't start blaming others for this. Instead, look at what is really causing your short-temperedness and try to get that fixed. Stress could be one underlying cause, and being more agreeable could be the best way to curb that stress.

BUSINESS - Don't Push Your Luck

You tend to be forward and pushy this month, and this could rub some people up the wrong way. You're probably not in the best frame of mind to meet outsiders if you're hoping to impress them. Not the best of times to pitch for new jobs or to make a good first impression. With those you already work with, you have a tendency to push your luck, but there's only so far you can go before you get an adverse reaction. Your criticisms can be hard to take and if you keep dishing it out don't be surprised if some of your best workers walk out on you. Control your temper this month and be more sensitive to the feelings of others.

You'll find your luck starts to improve the minute you change your approach to a more positive one.

LOVE & RELATIONSHIPS - Be Civilized

While all may start well in love, your angry disposition is enough to change things with the snap of a finger. The quarrelsome chi in your chart, if not kept in check, could unleash a destructive force in your relationships, and if you don't watch it, some words could be uttered that could have a devastating and lasting effect. As long as you are aware of this danger, you can take steps to avoid this happening. Carry the **Ping Peace Keychain** to help control your negative emotions.

Don't get suspicious of the people who care most about you. If you conjure up a bad scenario in your mind, you could create your own worst nightmare. Keep only positive thoughts in your head. Give your partner the benefit of the doubt. If you need to talk, talk, but be civilized about it. Behave like an adult if you want to be treated like one.

This is definitely no time to pursue a new romance. Also a **bad time** for getting married or getting engaged.

211

TWELFTH MONTH
Jan 6th - Feb 3rd 2013

DON'T LET THE WEATHER GET YOU DOWN OR YOU COULD FEEL MISERABLY ILL

The end of the Dragon Year brings the illness star back into your chart, making you more susceptible to falling ill and to catch straying bugs and diseases. You're weaker than usual, so do try to lead as healthy a lifestyle as you can and watch what you eat. Do get enough rest each night if you want to stay healthy. While there may be plenty to get done at work, pace yourself. If you plan well, you will have enough time to complete all tasks you're responsible for and still have time for yourself. Those of you with hobbies you enjoy should make some time to indulge yourself. This will help clear your mind and make you more effective at the workplace. It will also make you more agreeable in your relationships with others.

WORK & CAREER - Draining
You're prone to feeling tired and drained, especially those of you who have to put in long hours. Be sure to get enough rest. If your work is affecting your

health, think seriously about how you can change your daily schedule to improve things. What starts of as a minor ailment could develop into something bigger and more serious if you do not do anything about it. The illness star in your chart is exacerbated by the misfortune star in your sector. Counter this will the Metal element by wearing gold jewellery.

BUSINESS - Take a Break
Not a great month ahead for the Dragon in business. Although not all doom and gloom, it might appear so, because even the smallest crisis could become magnified when you are feeling under the weather. Your frame of mind is not attuned to coping with obstacles and difficulties and you'd probably much rather be on holiday, which could actually be the best thing for you right now. If you can afford to, treat yourself to a vacation or at least a weekend getaway. This will give your give your body a chance to rejuvenate and your mind a much-needed rest.

LOVE & RELATIONSHIPS - Be Pampered
You're feeling out of sorts with your energy levels ebbing at their lowest point. Do make it a point to get home from work early and to get some much-needed rest if you don't want the whole month to turn out simply disastrous. There's nothing more

213

miserable than falling seriously sick, and there is risk of that if you don't look after your health. Your love life is probably limping along awkwardly unless you can find yourself a lover who enjoys playing doctor or nursemaid. Not a month to go gallivanting in search of dates or new love interests. The heart may be willing but you could find – embarrassingly so – that the body is not. For the married Dragon, let your better half pamper you and use this opportunity to bond with one another. It might not be bonding on a very passionate level, but it will be comforting and heartwarming, and perhaps what the relationship needed.

EDUCATION - Be Careful with Sports

Be careful with your health, but also with physical sports this month. There is risk of injury to the neck, so do wear a helmet if engaging in activities that suggest their use. Don't take any risks; in fact, it may be a good idea to avoid activities that are overly physically strenuous for this month, until the afflicted illness star blows over. When studying, be sure to take regular breaks. Don't stress yourself out too much. Make sure you treat yourself to things that improve the way you feel, whether by hanging out with friends or engaging in a hobby you enjoy. All work and no play won't improve your grades.

Chapter Six

PROTECTING YOUR TRINITY OF LUCK USING SPIRITUAL FENG SHUI

In recent years, the need to incorporate the vital Third Dimension into the practice of feng shui has become increasingly urgent - as we observe the unbalanced energies of the world erupt in earthquakes, giant tsunamis, volcanic explosions, fierce winds, snowstorms and raging forest fires. It seems as if the four elements of the cosmic environment which control the forces of Nature are taking turns to unleash their fearsome wrath on the world, in the process also generating fierce emotions of anger and desperation that elicit killing violence. Last year the threat of nuclear radiation poisoning the world's atmosphere, its winds and waters also became potentially a fearsome reality. The world watched as Japan suffered - it was a big wakeup call!

So what are the four elements of the cosmic environment? These are fire and water, earth and wind. These four elements signify the cosmic forces of the Third Dimension in feng shui; these forces are powerful but they are not caused by some evil being out to wreak revenge or death on the inhabitants of the world.

What they are, are highly visual manifestations of the severe imbalances of energy that need to be righted, and the process of rebalancing causes millions of litres of water to get displaced, hence the severe rainfalls and the tsunamis. They cause thousands of miles of earth to get shifted, hence earthquakes and volcanic eruptions, which in turn causes winds in the upper atmosphere and the currents of the seas to go awry. Temperatures blow very hot and very cold… and pockets of the world's population experience suffering, loss and depravation!

In 2010 and 2011, the onslaught of natural and manmade disasters befalling the world were reflected in the feng shui and destiny charts of those years, and the revelations of the charts of 2012 suggest a need to use spiritual feng shui to find solutions, seek safeguards and use protection to navigate through these turbulent years; to be prepared… so to speak.

In their great wisdom, the ancient Masters had somehow devised specific methods, rituals and almost magical ways to safely live through disastrous times. For of course these natural calamities have repeated themselves - in a series of cyclical patterns - over thousands of years. We know that the world's energies work in repeating patterns and that there are cycles of change which affect our wellbeing.

To cope with these dangerous forces, it is necessary to decipher the charts, analyze the destructive forces revealed in the patterns of annual elements and then to apply cosmic remedies and transcendental cures - all part of the Third Dimension that completes our practice of feng shui. To enhance our trinity of luck i.e. our Heaven, Earth and Mankind luck.

In practicing spiritual feng shui, we look to generate good mankind luck, the luck we directly create for ourselves. The Buddhists and the Hindus call this luck generating good KARMA... and this is a concept that can be found in many of the world's spiritual practices.

Karma suggests that we can improve our luck, increase our longevity and experience happiness by purifying karmic debts and creating good merit through the practice of kindness, compassion and generosity. These are the basics. Thus we discovered through the years that our feng shui work and advice always worked best when we mindfully input genuinely kind motivations.

This led us to start using rituals of purification and appeasement to keep the four elements of fire, water, earth and wind balanced around our places of living and working. We discovered that there were direct correlations between the four elements of the cosmic world and the five elements of the human world.

Different animal signs are ruled by different elements at different times. Here we found that in time dimension feng shui - analyzing the annual and monthly charts to study the movement of element energy over time, spiritual methods played a big part in helping us improve our use of appeasement and purification rituals. They helped us to bridge the divide between the cosmic worlds - the spiritual worlds that existed alongside ours, and to add so much to our practice of feng shui. Included in the practice of Third Dimension spiritual feng shui are rituals and vocal incantations that can quell imbalances of energy.

There are powerful prayers and special offerings that can be used to invoke the aid of the cosmic beings of our space, the local landlords who rule our environment; the spirits and protectors who can assist us subdue the angry earth, control the raging waters, and basically keep us safe, making sure we will not be in the wrong place at the wrong time, that somehow we will change our plans, delay our travels or just stay home during crucial times when the elements of the world will be out of sync and raging.

Spiritual feng shui brings the practice of feng shui into other realms of existence. It addresses parallel world(s) that exist alongside ours; cosmic worlds inhabited by beings we call Spirits, local Landlords, protectors or even Deities who have supremacy over the elements.

There are Earth deities and Wind deities, Water and Fire Gods - in the old lineage texts of the ancient masters, references are made to the Four Direction Guardians, the heavenly kings who protect the four directions, North, South, East and West corners of our world, of the Eight Direction Goddesses who subdue destructive forces of wind and water and protect mankind. Much of the information related to these powerful cosmic deities has become the stuff of legends but they are real; and it is not difficult to invoke the assistance of these cosmic beings. It would be a big mistake to dismiss them as mere superstition!

Included here are some of the easier methods of spiritual feng shui which just about anyone can indulge in without compromising your belief systems. Always perform these practices with good motivation which is to keep your family safe, and your life humming along without success blocking obstacles.

You will notice that the use of symbolism activated by the mind's concentrated power is extremely potent, as are the purifying and offering rituals. One of the most effective way of staying safe and secure in your world is to make and wear special magic diagrams that incorporate sacred symbols and incantations or mantras into what we collectively refer to as amulets.

This practice is usually referred to as transcendental feng shui and the methods are shamanic, totally magical in their effect. The amulet can be customized to benefit different animal signs directly, incorporating the energizing symbols and syllables most beneficial to their elements in any given year. The amulet for the Dragon is given in this chapter here.

Spiritual feng shui also involves identifying the special Deity who has the greatest affinity with specific animal signs - these can be viewed as your Guardian Bodhisattva, similar to the patron saint or spiritual guide of each animal sign.

When you invite your Guardian Bodhisattva into your home, make offerings and recite their relevant mantra, you will benefit from the full force of their protective power. They will not only ensure that you stay safe and protected but will also multiply the potency of your time and space feng shui updates as well.

Incense Offerings
to Appease Local Protectors

Everyone benefits from learning how to make incense offerings on a regular basis to communicate directly with the "local landlords" that reside alongside us in our home space, on our street, in our town or village or sometimes on separate floors of high rise buildings. There is no need to be scared of them or to fear them. Most will leave human tenants alone.

When incense is offered to them, it creates the element of gratitude on their part; that is when they could assist you in whatever requests you make. It is not a widely known fact, but Spirit beings of the cosmic realm are always hungry, and at their lowest levels, they are known as hungry ghosts. The problem is that they are unable to eat! They cannot swallow food as their necks are said to be extremely narrow and the only way they can appease their hunger is by smelling aromatic, pungent incense which is yummy to them.

But just burning the incense alone is not as effective as reciting 21 times the blessing incantation that transforms the incense into sustenance for them, and then it is like giving them a feast, and the stronger the scent is, the tastier it will be to them.

There are so many auspicious benefits to preparing and then burning this incense offering in the outside space of your home, and also in the inside space by moving round each room three times in a clockwise direction. Done once a week on your *Day of Obstacles*, the incense will chase out all negativities and cleanse your home of bad energy. The local spirits will then also attract success, good health and wellbeing. Whatever disharmony there is in the home will quickly dissolve and all the afflictions of the year will also dissipate.

For the Dragon person, the best day to perform this incense offering ritual is **every Thursday**. And the best time would be to do it around **7 a.m. to 9 a.m.** in the morning.

In the old days, practitioners would burn freshly-cut juniper on hot charcoal and this gives off a very pleasant aroma together with white smoke which is also very pleasing to the spirits. This method continues to be used by the mountain people such as the Sherpas of the Himalayan mountain regions. If you go trekking in Nepal, you will see all along the trekking routes examples of these incense offering rituals, which are done to appease the local protectors hence keeping both visiting trekkers as well as the local people safe.

It is said that the more undeveloped a place is, the greater the presence of local spirits. Mountainous places are great favorites with the beings of the cosmic world. This is why those who go mountain climbing should always wear amulets to keep them safe from being harmed by some naughty wandering spirits.

Today however, especially if you live in the city, it is more convenient to use specially formulated incense pellets which burn easily and which give off a beautiful pungent aroma. The Malays and the Indians in Malaysia call this *kemenyen* and the Chinese sometimes use sandalwood incense powder to achieve the same effect.

Offering incense is one of the best ways to appease the local spirits of the land.

Use a special incense burner that comes with a handle and as you light the incense recite prayers that consecrate the incense so that it becomes easier for the spirits to enjoy the offering incense. Remember to take a humble attitude when making the offering and if you are a Buddhist, you can also take refuge in the triple gems before you start. The incantation mantra, to be recited at least 21 times, is:

NAMAH SARVA TATHAGATA AVALOKITE OM SAMBHARA SAMBHARA HUNG

Then think that you are making offering of the incense to the landlords and protectors of your house, your street and your neighborhood. You can think that they are accepting the incense and then you can request for specific illness or obstacles to be removed.

Those born in the year of the Dragon should request for protection against their five yellow affliction of 2012.

Customized Amulets to Protect Dragon's Afflicted Energies in 2012

There is a group of 102 Protective Amulets, reportedly first made in the Tibetan Nyingma monastery of Samye, the monastery in Tibet founded by the powerful Tibetan Lotus Born Buddha known as Guru Padmasambhava or Guru Rinpoche that is designed according to astrological calculations using the Chinese calendar i.e. based on the 60 year cycle of 12 animal signs and 5 elements.

Feng shui astrology attributes different influences arising from the different combinations that occur between the 12 animals and the 5 elements each year; these combinations of influences reveal the nuances of good and bad luck according to the year of birth.

Every sign requires different syllables, symbols and invocations, which subdue bad influences facing the sign. The amulet customized to the animal sign also promotes all-round good influences to come your way; it protects your property, business and work interests, and your family and loved ones.

226

Worn close to the body or placed near you near you, it increases your prosperity and keeps you safe from wandering spirits, which you might inadvertently encounter.

Amulet of the Fire Element

The Dragon benefits from wearing what is referred to as the Fire Amulet; and it is one shared with the other Earth signs of the Zodiac, the Ox, the Dog and the Sheep. The amulet is usually drawn as a circle sometimes signifying the underbelly of a protective tortoise. To the Tibetans, the tortoise signifies the protector of the Universe.

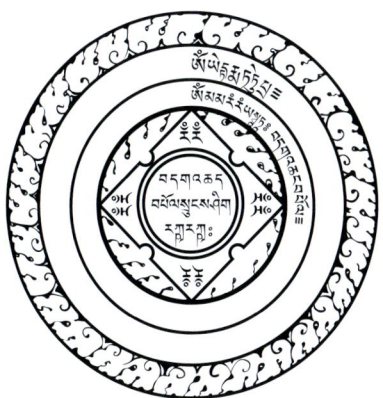

The Fire Amulet benefits the Dragon-born. Just having this amulet near you will protect you against harm and bad luck.

The centre of the circle is inscribed with invocations of safety and protection. A rough sketch of this amulet is shown here and this amulet works equally for the other three earth signs.

The Dragon belongs to the Earth element, so Fire energy will strengthen Dragon's intrinsic element. And in 2012 when the Dragon's chi strength is quite low and there are also afflictive stars circling the 24 Mountains, it is extremely beneficial to wear or carry this amulet. It should be written in red cinnamon ink on dark red or yellow paper or silk, then folded and kept in a suitable casing and worn near to the body.

Worn touching the body, especially if the amulet has been suitably consecrated, it can block off all adverse forces, and keep all planetary afflictions subdued. The amulet for the Dragon can be kept inside a leather or metal pouch. In 2012, the Metal element signifies power and influence, so having a gold or silver casing is appropriate.

We have also incorporated other amulets into a silk neck scarves suitable for dressing up your outfit while it watches over you at the same time. The amulets have a series of three concentric circles of mantras with an eight petalled lotus in the centre.

The Dragon can also wear auspicious wishfulfilling amulets as well especially those with the mantra of the Goddess Tara or with the special mantra that fulfils all your wishes:

OM PADMO USHNISHA BIMALE HUM PEH

Clear Crystal Ball with Empowered Golden Elephant Inside to Safeguard Dragon's Inner Essence

Those born in the year of the Dragon should always have clear crystal balls in the living area or in the centre of their homes. Crystal balls foster harmony in the home for everyone and also smoothes out every aspect of life's many dimensions for residents.

The Dragon benefits from all kinds of round crystal balls, but a crystal ball with a Golden Elephant within is even better as it will safeguard Dragon's inner essence in 2012.

For the Dragon, the crystal ball also enhances its intrinsic Earth energy. The circular shape is most auspicious and the solid crystal of the ball keeps everyone fully and solidly grounded. In 2012, the Earth element also signifies wealth and prosperity luck, and hence benefits all those Dragons wanting to focus on this aspect of their luck aspirations. If you can also find a crystal globe with a golden elephant inside, it will be even more auspicious for the Dragon as 2012 is your year.

Wish Granting Gem Tree for Wealth Creation Luck

The 2012 paht chee chart reveals the presence of one pillar where the elements are in a productive relationship. The month pillar shows yang Water producing yang Wood, and with the presence of the lap chun in this year's calendar, it means that there will be rejuvenated productive energy during the year. This will bring about excellent new growth.

To activate this, it is very beneficial to display a young tree of wealth that is in full bloom and which also represents a new beginning so a tree that is usually associated with the season of Spring is quite ideal. This is a feng shui enhancing symbol that is suitable for everyone.

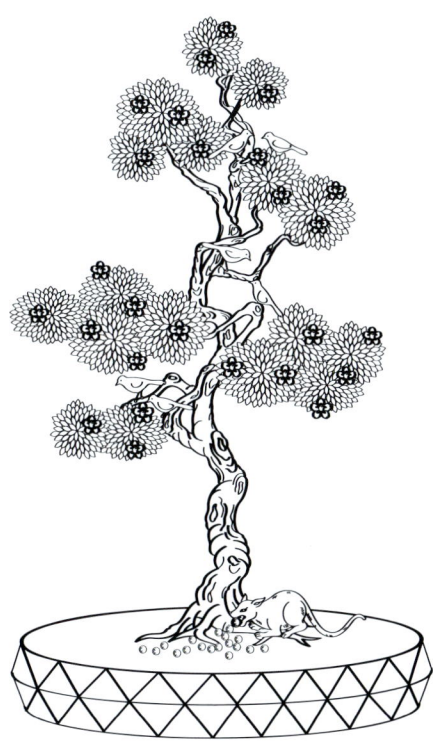

The wishgranting tree brings wonderful
growth energy for the Dragon, and activates the
productive month pillar in the year's Paht Chee.

Rising Blue Dragon to Magnify Luck from Heaven

The year's chart also reveals the importance of tapping effectively into the year's beautiful heaven luck. The centre of the feng shui chart is governed by the number 6, which apart from a being an auspicious white number is also representative of Big Metal and an abundance of heaven luck. Activating heaven luck not only attracts power and influence into your life, but good fortune luck also comes unexpectedly. Heaven luck is an important component of the trinity of luck and in 2012, harvesting the year's store of heaven luck energy is what will boost your feng shui luck.

The way to do this is to simulate the mighty Water Dragon of the year looking upwards into the skies getting ready to fly into a clear blue sky with the sunshine sending rays of yang chi all round.

Displayed on a sideboard in the centre of the home, this taps into the powerful energy of the Dragon. For the Dragon, the presence of the Dragon image in the home brings a double benefit as this is also your own sign. Tapping into the energy of the Dragon enhances the energy of the year.

Golden Power Wheel
Powerful Symbol of Upward Mobility for the Dragon in 2012

The Golden Power Wheel can help the Dragon activate promotion luck, and having it near your place of work will enhance your chances of upward mobility. Display the spinning wealth wheel which is created from two circular brass plates that are inscribed with the powerful mandalas of the male and female wealth Gods of the cosmic traditions.

Each side has eight images within the eight petals of a stylised lotus. These images of wealth gods and goddesses are placed facing each other, and when the plates are turned, the energy released from the wealth deities being pleased, attracts prosperity into the home or office. Behind the Male Deities are the eight auspicious signs and in the centre the seed syllable Hum; behind the female Deities are the royal emblems and in the centre the seed syllable *Hrih*.

Do take note that this is a sacred representation of the Wealth Deities, so they also bring wealth luck. It is an excellent idea to spin this Golden Power Wheel at least once a day. Do place the wheel on a high level i.e. on a sideboard rather than on a low coffee table.

Fire Totem Talisman Pendant to Safeguard Long Term Prospects

One of the most popular ways of wearing several auspicious cosmic symbols together is to use the totem concept which groups three or more powerful instruments or symbols stacked one on top of another. Totems make powerful talismans when they are correctly made and properly energized with special incantations.

Cosmic totems that put together element groups of protective sacred symbols can be excellent for compensating for a vital missing element. In 2012, the Fire element signified by the color red is required to bring about a proper balance to the energies of the world; but more than that, 2012 is the kind of year when it is extremely beneficial to invoke the powerful Bodhisattva and deity guardians of the Earth, many of whom are associated with *sanskrit* syllables.

The Fire Totem Pendant comprises three powerful sanskrit syllables - at the base is *Bam*, followed by *Ah*, and then *Hrih* at the top. These syllables are strongly associated with the Tibetan spiritual traditions and the shamans of pre-Buddhist Tibet wear these syllables to keep them safe and empowered at all times. But these syllables are also used as wish-granting aids in powerful spiritual visualisations.

The syllable Hrih is a very powerful symbol which protects and also sends out a great deal of loving energy. It makes the wearer appear softer, warmer and kinder. The Fire Totem Talisman is a pendant made completely of gold which can be worn touching the throat chakra. Not many know it but the throat chakra is red in color and it governs the power of one's speech.

Anyone wanting their spoken words, their speech, their selling proposals and so on to become empowered can wear this totem pendant.

If you work in a profession where the way you talk, give a speech, make a proposal and otherwise use your voice is crucial, then this totem pendant is ideal for you. Those in the teaching profession, in law and in the entertainment industry, for instance, would benefit greatly from wearing it.

There is a lotus and an utpala flower joining these seed syllables - and all the five items in the totem are related to the Fire energy of red. The color red signifies the Fire element. The lotus signifies purity and the utpala flower suggests the attainment of great wisdom. This is a very powerful emblem not just for protection but more importantly for empowerment. When you wear them, think that they exude rays of red light radiating outwards from you in all directions.

Invoking Dragon's Guardian Protector Samantabhadra Sitting on a White Elephant

The Dragon's Bodhisattva Guardian is Samantabadra, the Deity that sits on the White Elephant that has so many powerful attributes.

For the Dragon, this is a very special deity indeed and inviting the presence of Samantabhadra into your home or into your work space can be most beneficial. Look for an image that " speaks" to you and then invite the image into your home. Just having the presence in the home is symbolically powerful especially if placed in the Southeast, the Dragon's home location.

Place offerings of water bowls, candles and food to establish a "connection", and each time you make incense offering to the local landlords and environmental spirits, do include your Guardian Deity by name in your list of recipients.

It is a good idea to make the dedication to your Guardian Deity first. This need not be a very elaborate ritual. The key to success in incorporating spiritual feng shui into your daily life is to be very relaxed and joyous about all that you do.

What is beneficial about having your Guardian Deity in your home is that the spirits of the cosmic world always respect the Bodhisattvas and Buddhas, and when you invoke their protection, it offers you safe refuge from being harmed by the spirits that may be residing in your space.

237

So What Do You Think?

We hope you enjoyed this book and gained some meaningful insights about your own personal horoscope and animal sign. This book, if used properly and regularly, is a goldmine of feng shui knowledge… so hopefully you are already feeling a difference and enjoying the results of positive actions you have taken.

But Don't Stop Now!

You can receive the latest weekly news and even more feng shui updates from Lillian herself absolutely FREE! Learn even more of her secrets and open your mind to the deeper possibilities of feng shui today.

Lillian Too's FREE online weekly ezine is now AVAILABLE!

Here's how easy it is to subscribe. Just go online to: *www.lilliantoomandalaezine.com* and sign up today!

Your newsletter will be delivered automatically
to your inbox each week

....

You will receive a special FREE BONUS from Lillian when
you subscribe to Lillian's FREE Mandala Weekly Ezine…
but it's only available to those who register online at:
www.lilliantoomandalaezine.com

....

Once you register for the weekly newsletter,
you become eligible for special discounts and offers only
available to ezine subscribers!

....

DON'T BE LEFT OUT! JOIN TODAY!

Thanks again for investing in yourself and in this book.
Now join me online every week and learn how easy it really
is to make good feng shui a way of life!

Lillian's online FREE weekly ezine is only available when
you register online at *www.lilliantoomandalaezine.com*